RUSSIA AND THE KYOTO PROTOCOL

Opportunities and Challenges

Edited by Anna Korppoo,
Jacqueline Karas
and Michael Grubb

 CHATHAM HOUSE

Published in Great Britain in 2006 by
The Royal Institute of International Affairs,
Chatham House, 10 St James's Square, London SW1Y 4LE
(Charity Registration No. 208 223).

British Library Cataloguing in Publication Data
A CIP catalogue record for this book is available from the British Library.

ISBN 1 86203 168 1 *paperback*

Cover design by Matthew Link
Typeset in Bembo by Koinonia
Printed and bound in Great Britain by Nuffield Press

*Chatham House (The Royal Institute of International Affairs) is an
independent body which promotes the rigorous study of international
questions and does not express opinions of its own. The opinions
expressed in this publication are the responsibility of the authors.*

CONTENTS

FIGURES, TABLES AND BOXES

Figures

Tables

Boxes

FOREWORD

The Kyoto Protocol 'seeks to address the most challenging of global environmental problems' and is 'without precedent in international affairs. … Specific legal commitments capping emissions of such gases by each industrialized country constitute an achievement that many political sceptics had dismissed only months before [the adoption of the protocol] as impossible.' So wrote my predecessor as Programme Head, Michael Grubb, in his preface to the *Kyoto Protocol: A Guide and Assessment*, published by Chatham House in 1999. And yet, by summer 2004, it looked as if this landmark treaty might be consigned to historical oblivion. This changed dramatically in September 2004, when the Russian government submitted the ratification document to the State Duma. Russian ratification finally brought the treaty into force in February 2005 and thereby fundamentally changed the terms of the international debate on climate change. The focus is now firmly on implementation of current commitments and building on those for the future.

Chatham House's Energy, Environment and Development Programme seeks to influence the international debate on sustainable development, so as to achieve better-informed decision-making. Thus our interest in examining Russian ratification and implementation of the Kyoto Protocol is not purely historical, but is aimed at drawing out lessons for today's policy-makers who are involved in further developing the international climate regime. Indeed, Russia can in many ways be considered a test case and possible model for future international deals, in that it is classified as a developed country in the Protocol, but unlike other developed countries it has a large surplus emissions quota to sell. Like many developed countries, it faces major challenges in making its domestic energy market efficient, although the scale of the problems in Russia tends to be larger. But Russia is also plagued by some of the generic problems that are prevalent in developing countries, such as an

inefficient bureaucracy and corruption. Accordingly, this book not only tells the story of Russian ratification, but also assesses Russian climate policy and the implications for those engaging in carbon market transactions with Russia – with an eye towards what all this means for the future international climate change regime.

Of course, Russia's decision to ratify the Protocol was not a spontaneous one. It was the culmination of a complex internal political process, combined with dialogues on various issues with external actors. The final bargain involved climate policy considerations as well as international trade policy and domestic energy concerns. This bundling of issues was necessary to break through various log jams, and was based on creative diplomacy. Future developments in the international climate regime are expected to seek to reduce emissions substantially, which will place stresses on all countries, although the implications will be different for each country. Therefore, the negotiating agenda can be expected to become ever more complex and broad-ranging as the process intensifies. The environmental objectives will need to be squared with ensuring energy needs are met, minimizing harm to international competitiveness, and taking measures to adapt to climate change – all within a framework that must be equitable if it is to be legitimate. This is a very tall order. A better understanding of the decision-making processes at work within key countries – which this book attempts to achieve in the case of Russia – is a theme that Chatham House will continue to pursue in the coming years. Indeed, I expect that we will continue to collaborate with other organizations, both governmental and non-governmental, as we move forward with this research.

This book is a continuation of activity that Chatham House has undertaken on climate change policy in Russia since 1998, which itself was based on Chatham House's long-standing engagement on Russian energy policy, going back decades. On climate policy, Chatham House developed a series of activities both in Moscow and London that sought to enhance understanding of the Russian approach to climate change policy. Chatham House then began exploring the prospects for Russian ratification of the Protocol in summer 2003, work that culminated in an expert workshop in March 2004 entitled 'Russia and the Kyoto Protocol: Opportunities and Challenges'. The aim was to better understand the factors at work in Russia, not only from a climate policy perspective, but

in the context of Russia's broader foreign policy objectives and institutions. This book draws on and updates that work.

The book would not have been possible without the support of several partners. The interface with the Cambridge Economic Policy Associates (CEPA) was especially important, in particular their work on the costs and benefits to the Russian Federation of the Kyoto Protocol which provided the basis for part of the Chatham House expert workshop in March 2004.

I am very grateful to the editors, Anna Korppoo, Jacqueline Karas, and Michael Grubb, who personally invested above and beyond the available resources to make this book a reality. Colleagues in Chatham House also gave much of their time and energy to this project: the Russia and Eurasia Programme helpfully contributed their expertise on Russian foreign policy-making; Margaret May, head of the Publications Department, cheerfully supported and guided us forward during all stages of this process; and Lorraine Howe, manager of the Energy, Environment and Development Programme, anchored this work valiantly throughout.

Finally, this book is part of a rich tradition within the Programme of carrying out research on many aspects of the international climate regime. In this context, I pay tribute to the Programme's governmental and corporate sponsors, as well as to the many distinguished researchers and Associate Fellows who have grounded our work on climate change.

Richard Tarasofsky
Head, Energy, Environment and
Development Programme
Chatham House

ACKNOWLEDGMENTS

This book would not have been possible without the support of several partners, and especially Cambridge Economic Policy Associates (CEPA), whose 2004 study *Costs and Benefits to the Russian Federation of the Kyoto Protocol* provided the basis for four of the chapters. The editors are very grateful to the other members of the CEPA project team, Jonathan Mirrlees-Black, Nebojša Novčić and David Newbery.

Similarly, the editors wish to thank Chatham House for hosting a workshop on the topic in March 2004, on which a number of the chapters draw, and the journal *Energy Policy* for granting permission to reprint a slightly updated version of the article 'Russian energy efficiency projects: lessons learnt from the Activities Implemented Jointly pilot phase'. Specific appreciation goes to the government JI/CDM programmes of the Netherlands, Austria, Sweden, Germany and Denmark for their assistance with material collection, and to informants involved in the AIJ projects implemented and planned in Russia by the Dutch, Swedish, German, US and Finnish governments.

The editors and authors are particularly grateful to Oleg Pluzhnikov of the Russian Ministry of Economic Development and Trade, Alexey Kokorin of WWF Russia, Vitaly Matsarsky of the UNFCCC and George Safonov of the Moscow Higher School of Economics, who all provided invaluable insights into the Russian perspective on the key issues. Similarly, the book benefited greatly from the input of participants in the study group convened in Bonn in May 2005 to discuss the draft text, including John Drexhage of IISD, Sarah Hendry of DEFRA, Taishi Sugiyama of CRIEPI and Vitaly Matsarsky. Specific thanks also go to Professor Malcolm Hill of Loughborough University Business School for providing structural comments on the draft text. Thanks also to Bobo Lo and James Nixey of Chatham House's Russia and Eurasia Programme for their expert insights on aspects of this work.

Further thanks to those experts who freely shared their knowledge and views with the editors and contributors: Vladimir Berdin (Russian National Pollution Abatement Facility), Stepan Dudarev (National Carbon Union), Inna Gritsevich (Centre for Energy Efficiency), Alexander Khanykov (National Carbon Sequestration Foundation – NCSF), Miia Kinnunen and Jyrki Luukkanen (Finland Futures Research Centre), Chatham House Associate Fellow John Mitchell, Elena Nikitina (Russian Academy of Sciences), Erik Mielke (Dresdner Kleinwort Wasserstein), Justin Mundy (Deutsche Bank), Mihail Rogankov of the (then) Energy Carbon Facility of RAO UES Rossii, Larisa Skuratovskaya (Russian Academy of the Medical Sciences), Chatham House Associate Fellow Jonathan Stern, Evgeny Sokolov (NCSF), Michael Yulkin (Environmental Investment Centre), and the Climate Strategies Green Investment Scheme project team.

The support of Chatham House staff was vital to this project. Lorraine Howe and Gemma Green provided brilliant administrative support, Nick Jones prepared figures and tables, and Margaret May and Matthew Link oversaw the editing, production and publication. The editors also extend their appreciation to Alexey Kokorin of WWF Russia for organizing the Russian translation of this book and to Larisa Skuratovskaya of the Institute of General Pathology of the Russian Academy of the Medical Sciences for the translation of related Briefing Notes.

Finally this book would not have been possible without the financial support of a number of governments and companies. In particular, the editors thank DEFRA for their support for the CEPA report, the Chatham House workshop and this publication. The financial support of the Foreign and Commonwealth Office UK and British Petroleum for this book is gratefully acknowledged. The Academy of Finland funded key research hosted by the Turku School of Economics and Business Administration, and earlier funding by the Fortum Foundation also supported this project. The governments and businesses which provide the core support for Chatham House's Energy, Environment and Development Programme are also acknowledged.

Last but not least, the editors thank their ever patient and supportive partners and spouses Mike Hugh, David Lye and Joanna Depledge.

As ever, responsibility for the content remains with the editors and contributors.

PREFACE: THE NEW RUSSIAN ENIGMA

Observers of Russian involvement in the international negotiations on climate change, which date back to 1991, might well be led to the same conclusion as Winston Churchill, who famously remarked that predicting what action Russia would take was 'a riddle wrapped in a mystery inside an enigma'.[1]

From an observer's perspective, Russia's involvement in the development of the 1992 UN Framework Convention on Climate Change (UNFCCC) was confined mostly to trying to maintain its status among the industrialized countries while protecting the special circumstances of 'economies in transition'. In 1996, Russia allied with most of OPEC in opposing the Geneva Declaration, in which most of the rest of the world endorsed the basic principles that led to the Kyoto Protocol. But during the following year, in response to both strenuous efforts by the US and the evolving design of the Protocol during its negotiation, Russia came to a more positive view of the negotiations, and in the final stages succeeded in securing an emission allowance which permits it to return its (drastically reduced) emissions to 1990 levels during the first commitment period (2008–12).

After the US withdrawal, most observers judged that the Protocol was still fundamentally in Russia's interests. Few, if any, predicted that Russia – which now held the keys to entry into force – would become the focus of international concerns in the midst of repeatedly contradictory signals about its intent. As in the Cold War, Kremlin-watching once again became a topic of endless fascination. Russia's eventual decision to ratify brought relief to many, yet even the most senior sources in the West still profess uncertainty as to what finally clinched the decision and its timing, with different groups and initiatives claiming credit for making the crucial breakthroughs.

This book sheds some light upon these issues, but is primarily focused

upon learning lessons, looking forward, and understanding the implications. With the decision made and the Kyoto Protocol in force, what now? Does ratification mark a decisive break with the hesitant engagement of the past, or was it a convenience that does not fundamentally change the underlying dynamic of caution and suspicion? What are the opportunities, and where are the pitfalls? Will Russia resolve its internal conflicts and become a credible partner in implementing the pact, or will internal divergences and institutional confusion remain the hallmark of Russian engagement on climate change? This book lays out estimates of the potential benefits to Russia of the 'Kyoto mechanisms', but given the difficult history, will they be important in relation to foreign investment in Russian energy or will they remain a puny sideshow? Indeed, does climate change or the Kyoto Protocol really matter to Russia at all? These and related questions form the core of this book.

The book's editors and contributors have considerable experience of working with Russian partners on climate change and have benefited from extensive discussion with Russian colleagues, but it unavoidably remains a foreign perspective. The evidence collated, however, does illustrate core themes that both Russia, and other countries, ignore at their peril.

Russia is a proud country, sensitive in the light of its former superpower status. It has never followed other countries' bidding, and indeed the pressure exerted by European environmental ministries was at times probably quite counterproductive – Russia may respond to engagement, but not yield to pressure on an issue that is seen to be bound up with the prospects for its core economic sector. Climate policy has only made headway when set constructively in the context of other agendas, whether on international energy investments, the World Trade Organization or the higher-level diplomatic relationships with the EU and the UN and its organizations.

Engaging with Russia is a long-term business. Most of the companies now operating profitably in Russia do so on the back of very long-term involvement, usually including a number of hard and costly lessons along the way. The same is true for countries.

Excepting the US courtship of 1995–9, most pro-Kyoto countries paid insufficient attention to Russia during this period, and later paid the price in terms of delay and uncertainty over the treaty's entry into force.

While such countries made strenuous efforts in 2002–4 to engage with Russia, ratification may lead to a natural tendency to relax the effort and this could undermine much of what has been achieved. From the Russian perspective also, the potential gains from the Protocol could slip away if institutional gridlock in Russia leads potential partners preferentially to seek emission allowances from Ukraine, other east European countries or the Clean Development Mechanism.

Understanding remains scarce, and perceptions remain divergent. The situation after ratification is reminiscent of what happened when Russia – after considerable efforts by the US – signalled its willingness to consider linking emissions trading with 'green investment', at the Hague Conference of Parties to the UNFCCC in November 2000. For the next six months, Russia waited for a response, while its would-be partners waited for more details. Now that Russia has declared in favour of the Kyoto Protocol, it expects the promised investment to flow; meanwhile its would-be partners still wait for more clarity, transparency and certainty around the institutions of compliance and the ground rules for trade and investment. If each waits for the other to move, both will end up disappointed and frustrated.

Trust and understanding remain the commodities in shortest supply, and these cannot be picked up, or dropped, according to the needs of the hour. As indicated in the Foreword, this book itself is the product of long engagement by the authors on Russian issues. We hope that its publication will, in turn, help others to understand Russia better, and perhaps help give Russians more insight into how their country, and the international regime on climate change, are perceived by others. Only upon such improved and mutual understanding, along with growing investment through the mechanisms established, can trust ultimately be built.

Michael Grubb

EDITORS AND PRINCIPAL CONTRIBUTORS

Anna Korppoo is the author of several articles on Russian climate and energy policy, and worked as a coordinator and researcher in the Climate Strategies project on the Russian Green Investment Scheme in 2001–02. In 2000–03 she organized three international workshops in Moscow on Russian climate policy, the first of which was initiated by Chatham House. She has developed extensive contacts in the Russian climate change world and has followed the ratification process closely. She is currently a PhD student at Imperial College London, focusing on energy efficiency in Russian industry.

Jacqueline Karas is an Associate Fellow of the Energy, Environment and Development Programme at Chatham House and an independent consultant on climate change and sustainable development. She was previously a Research Fellow with the Sustainable Development Programme at Chatham House, with overall responsibility for work on climate change at Chatham House. A graduate in environmental sciences, she previously held positions at the Climatic Research Unit at the University of East Anglia, Friends of the Earth and the New Economics Foundation. Her research spans the science, impacts, policy and politics of climate change and related issues. Recent work covers prospects for – and evolution of – the international climate regime, political challenges of Russian ratification and emerging markets in emissions trading.

Michael Grubb is a leading international researcher on the economic dimensions of and policy responses to climate change and energy policy issues including renewable energy sources. He has been a lead author for several reports of the Intergovernmental Panel on Climate Change (IPCC) addressing the economic, technological and social aspects of limiting greenhouse gas emissions and has advised a number of govern-

ments, companies and international studies on climate change policy. He is editor-in-chief of the journal *Climate Policy* and is on the editorial board of *Energy Policy*. He was formerly Head of the Energy and Environmental Programme at Chatham House and remains an Associate Fellow of the Energy, Environment and Development Programme. He is now Chief Economist at the Carbon Trust and a Visiting Professor at Imperial College London, and is also a Senior Research Associate at the Faculty of Economics at Cambridge University. He gained his PhD in energy systems analysis from Cambridge.

Cambridge Economic Policy Associates (CEPA) is a UK-based economic and finance policy advisory business. Its focus is on issues where economics, finance and public policy overlap across a range of infrastructure sectors worldwide. CEPA advises governments and their agencies, regulators, non-governmental organizations and the private sector across three practice areas: (i) Emerging Markets, including developing and transition country markets; (ii) Regulatory Economics and Competition, focusing on UK and European markets; and (iii) Public Policy and Finance in the UK. In 2004 CEPA produced a study for the UK Department for Environment, Food and Rural Affairs (DEFRA) entitled *Costs and Benefits to the Russian Federation of the Kyoto Protocol,* which acts as a source for a number of chapters in this book. The CEPA team responsible for the study, which included Michael Grubb and Anna Korppoo, were:

Jonathan Mirrlees-Black
In his former capacity as Director of Cambridge Economic Policy Associates (CEPA)
Currently, Head of Utilities Research, Exane BNP Paribas

Nebojša Novčić
Consultant, Cambridge Economic Policy Associates (CEPA)

David Newbery
Vice-Chairman, Cambridge Economic Policy Associates (CEPA)
Professor of Applied Economics, University of Cambridge

OTHER CONTRIBUTORS

Alexey Kokorin
Coordinator of Climate and Energy Program
WWF Russia

Benito Müller
Senior Research Fellow, Oxford Institute for Energy Studies;
Associate Fellow, Chatham House

George Safonov
Director, Centre for Environmental Economics,
The State University - Higher School of Economics, Moscow

Authors and sources for individual chapters are as follows:

Chapter 1 by Michael Grubb with contributions from Anna Korppoo and Jacqueline Karas.

Chapter 2 by Jacqueline Karas and Anna Korppoo with contributions from Alexey Kokorin, partly based on Karas (2004).

Chapter 3 primarily sourced from CEPA (2004) and also based on Grubb (2004), with further research and revisions by Jacqueline Karas.

Chapter 4 by Jacqueline Karas, with contributions from Benito Müller (partly based on Müller 2004) and Anna Korppoo.

Chapter 5 primarily sourced from CEPA (2004), also based on Karas (2004) and Grubb (2003), with further contributions, research and revisions by Jacqueline Karas.

Chapter 6 analysis sourced from CEPA (2004), with further research and revisions by Jacqueline Karas.

Chapter 7 by Anna Korppoo, largely based on her work in CEPA (2004).

Chapter 8 revised by Anna Korppoo from Korppoo (2005) published in the journal *Energy Policy*.

Chapter 9 revised by Anna Korppoo from her work for CEPA (2004), also published as Korppoo (2004).

Chapter 10 by Anna Korppoo and Jacqueline Karas, with contributions from George Safonov.

Chapter 11 by Michael Grubb with contributions from Anna Korppoo and Jacqueline Karas.

GLOSSARY AND ABBREVIATIONS

AA   Assigned amount, the permitted emissions in CO_2e during a commitment period.

AAU   Assigned Amount Unit, the basic emission allowance for the industrialized countries listed in Annex B of the Kyoto Protocol. An AAU corresponds to one metric tonne of CO_2e which can be emitted any time during the first commitment period (2008–12), or banked for subsequent use.

Additionality The requirement that a project results in additional emissions savings, compared to those that would have occurred in the absence of the project, if it is to qualify as a JI or CDM project under the Kyoto Protocol. The additional emissions savings form the basis for issuing emissions credits.

AIJ   Activities Implemented Jointly, pilot phase of JI and the CDM.

Annex 1   Annex 1 to the UNFCCC lists industrialized-country and economy-in-transition parties to the UNFCCC that assume specific commitments.

Annex B   Annex B to the Kyoto Protocol defines emission allowances of Annex I countries for Kyoto's commitment period.

BaU   Business as usual, description generally applied to a scenario of what might have occurred in the absence of the Kyoto Protocol.

BCF   BioCarbon Fund of the World Bank

Bubble   An option that allows a group of countries to meet their targets jointly.

CDCF   Community Development Carbon Fund of the World Bank

CDM	The Clean Development Mechanism, defined by Article 12 of the Kyoto Protocol. Refers to the emission reduction activities implemented in Non-Annex 1, mainly developing, countries to create CERs, which can be used by Annex B countries to fulfil their commitments.
CEPA	Cambridge Economic Policy Associates
CER	Certified Emission Reduction, a unit issued pursuant to Article 12 of the Kyoto Protocol (the CDM).
CERT	Carbon Emission Reduction Trading model used by CEPA in this report.
CERUPT	Certified Emission Reduction Unit Procurement Tender – Dutch government programme to implement CDM by providing funds for acquisition of CERs.
CHP	Combined Heat and Power, synonymous with co-generation.
CICERO	Center for International Climate and Environmental Research, Oslo
CO_2	Carbon dioxide
CO_2e	Carbon dioxide equivalence, a measure of the emissions of a gas by weight, multiplied by its GWP.
COP	Conference of the Parties to the UNFCCC
COP/MOP	Conference of the Parties to the UNFCCC and Meeting of the Parties to the Kyoto Protocol
Early JI	The idea of crediting emission reduction projects other than under the CDM prior to the year 2008 by using contracts to transfer AAUs to honour the emission reductions generated by an early investment.
EBRD	European Bank for Reconstruction and Development
EET3	The non-EU east European transition economies – Bulgaria, Romania and Croatia.
EIT	Economy in transition, refers to former Soviet Union countries and central and east European countries.
Eligibility	Refers to a status when an Annex 1 country is qualified to participate in IET after fulfilling compliance requirements defined under the Marrakech Accords.
ERU	Emission Reduction Unit, a unit issued pursuant to Article 6 of the Kyoto Protocol (JI).

ERUPT — Emission Reduction Purchase Tender – Dutch government programme using the JI mechanism to acquire ERUs generated in host countries during the commitment period 2008–12 as part of the Dutch obligations under the terms of the Kyoto Protocol.

ET — Emissions trading, as defined by Art. 17 of the Kyoto Protocol, allows emitters (countries, companies or facilities) to buy or sell emission to other emitters.

EUA — EU Allowance, in use under the EU ETS.

EU ETS — European Union Emission Trading Scheme, a compulsory emissions trading scheme for EU member states.

EU-15 — The European Union during the Kyoto negotiations comprising 15 member states. Ten central and east European countries joined the EU in 2004, making the current EU-25.

FAS — Federal Anti-monopoly Service of Russia

FDI — Foreign direct investment

Fungibility — Interchangeability of AAUs, ERUs, CERs and RMUs in the Kyoto market.

GDP — Gross domestic product

GHG — Greenhouse gas. The Kyoto Protocol regulates a 'basket' of six GHGs:

CO_2 — carbon dioxide
CH_4 — methane
N_2O — nitrous oxide
HFCs — hydrofluorocarbons
PFCs — perfluorocarbons
SF_6 — sulphur hexafluoride

GEF — Global Environment Facility

GIS — Green Investment Scheme: the idea of recycling revenues from emissions trading to further GHG emission reductions or other environmental purposes in EITs.

GWP — Global warming potential, a measure of the warming effect of a substance relative to that of CO_2 over a given timescale (100 years in the case of the Kyoto Protocol).

Hot air — The excess emission allowances over the 'business as usual' emissions in the commitment period have been referred

	to as 'hot air'. This term is offensive to many in Russia.
IEA	International Energy Agency
IET	International Emissions Trading, as allowed under Article 17 of the Kyoto Protocol.
IPCC	Intergovernmental Panel on Climate Change; reviews scientific research and provides governments with summaries and advice on climate problems.
JI	Joint Implementation, defined by Article 6 of the Kyoto Protocol. Refers to the emission reduction activities implemented jointly between industrialized countries and EITs.
JUSSCANNZ	Group of Australia, Canada, Iceland, Japan, New Zealand, Norway, Russia, Switzerland, Ukraine and the US that emerged during the Kyoto negotiations.
kWh	Kilowatt hour
Linking Directive	EU directive linking the EU ETS with other flexible mechanisms under the Kyoto Protocol.
MEDT	Ministry of Economic Development and Trade of Russia
MES	Ministry of Education and Science of Russia
MIA	Ministry of International Affairs of Russia
MIE	Ministry of Industry and Energy of Russia
Minregion	Ministry of Regional Development of Russia
MNR	Ministry of Natural Resources of Russia
MOP	Meeting of the Parties to the Kyoto Protocol
MtCe	Mega (million) tonnes of carbon equivalent
MW	Megawatts
NAP	National Allocation Plan under the EU ETS
NAPR	Russian National Action Plan on Kyoto Protocol Implementation
NATO	North Atlantic Treaty Organization
NC	National Communication
NCSF	National Carbon Sequestration Foundation: organization of Russian businesses.
NCU	National Carbon Union, organization of Russian businesses interested in Kyoto-related activities.
NEFCO	Nordic Environment Finance Corporation
NGO	Non-Governmental Organization
Non-Annex 1	Parties to the UNFCCC not listed in the Annex 1 of the

	Kyoto Protocol: mostly developing countries but also several countries of the former Soviet Union. Non-Annex 1 countries do not have quantified emission reduction or limitation commitments so far.
OECD	Organization for Economic Cooperation and Development
OPEC	Organization of Petroleum Exporting Countries
PCF	Prototype Carbon Fund of the World Bank
PDD	Project Design Document
PIN	Project Idea Note
PPP	Purchasing Power Parity
RAO UES	Unified Energy System of Russia, Russian electricity monopoly.
RAS	Russian Academy of Science
RES	Russian Energy Strategy until the year 2020
RMU	Removal Unit, defined by the Marrakech Accords. Represents sink credits created by Annex I countries and can only be used during the commitment period in which they have been generated.
Roshydromet	Russian Federal Service for Hydrometeorology and Environmental Monitoring
Rosnauka	Federal Agency for Science and Innovation of Russia
Rosstroi	Federal Agency of Construction and Housing of Russia
SICLIP	Swedish International Climate Investment Programme
SNF	Foundation for Research in Economics and Business Administration
TACIS	EU technical assistance programme for countries of eastern Europe and Central Asia
tCO_2e	tonnes of GHG in terms of their (warming) equivalence to CO_2
TGF	Testing Ground Facility (Baltic Sea Region)
Track 1 JI	JI projects implemented when host country is in full compliance under the Kyoto Protocol.
Track 2 JI	A procedure for approving JI projects for host countries that have not fulfilled the general reporting requirements of the Marrakech Accords and therefore are not in full compliance under the Kyoto Protocol.

UNCED	UN Conference on Environment and Development, held in Rio de Janeiro in 1992.
UNDP	United Nations Development Programme
UNFCCC	United Nations Framework Convention on Climate Change
WCCC	World Climate Change Conference, held in Moscow in September 2003.
WEO	World Energy Outlook
WTO	World Trade Organization
WWF Russia	Russian office of WWF, an international conservation NGO.

1 INTRODUCTION

This book aims to contribute to understanding the past and potential role of Russia in international processes to tackle climate change. Russia's decision to ratify the Kyoto Protocol finally brought it into force on 16 February 2005. That event, fourteen years after negotiations began on the UN Framework Convention on Climate Change, has moved the world into a new phase in its response to climate change.

Russia's role in the negotiations has always been, and remains, enigmatic. That is not surprising. The negotiating process was born while Russia was in the throes of radical upheaval during the disintegration of the Soviet Union and the ensuing devastating economic decline which peaked in 1998. Russian engagement, perhaps more than that of any other country, has been impaired not only by this psychological legacy, but by the fact that few Russian negotiators were fluent in English. Anyone involved in international negotiations knows that simultaneous translation remains a poor substitute for the understanding that can arise through bilateral discourse in the corridors.

Russia's geographical, economic and geopolitical position also sets it uniquely apart. President Vladimir Putin's light-hearted comment at the Moscow World Climate Conference in October 2003 that 'a warmer world would mean Russians could spend less on their winter coats', with the qualification that 'we must think what consequences of these changes we will face in certain regions where there will be droughts and where there will be floods', encapsulated the reality of Russian debate about the pros and cons of a warming climate. Most scientists' belief that considerable climate change is probably unavoidable and that the negotiations are about how to slow it and avert its dangerous consequences is a subtlety not easily communicated in domestic debate.

Russia's energy endowments also put it in an ambiguous position. It is rich in all the hydrocarbons and the economy is heavily dependent on

energy exports. Set against the enormous potential for improving its energy efficiency and also possibly increasing exports of natural gas in a carbon-constrained world, the core fear of some in Russia is that carbon constraints might also constrain hydrocarbon usage and economic growth. This perspective would tend to align Russia economically and politically with some of the Organization of Petroleum Exporting Countries (OPEC) – almost irrespective of the other pros and cons of the treaty.

Geopolitically too, Russia has sat in an uneasy position. Since the dissolution of the Soviet Union Russia has frequently been closely linked with the US on international affairs. In the climate change negotiations Russia developed a core partnership with the US based around the need for international flexibility. This was institutionalized through the 'Umbrella Group' of industrialized countries opposed to the EU's less compromising environmental focus.[1] The US withdrawal from the Kyoto Protocol shattered the Umbrella Group at around the same time that the US–Russia relationship soured more generally, and Putin's rise helped to reassert Russia's independence. The slow and cautious development of the relationship between the EU and Russia is based firmly on their complementary interests in energy but is undermined by the enlargement of the EU and by Russia's sense of exclusion from key EU decision-making processes.

The central role of Russia in the treaty's final entry into force – and the complex and difficult path that led to that outcome – is an appropriate backdrop to the future, and is examined in detail in Chapter 2. Russia is by far the largest single emitter of greenhouse gases (GHG) among the industrialized countries now bound by the Kyoto Protocol, accounting for more than a quarter of the total Annex 1 country emissions after the US withdrawal. Moreover, given the collapse of its emissions in the course of its economic transition, Russia is the country with by far the largest potential surplus of emission allowances for sale under the Kyoto international trading mechanisms. It is also generally considered to be the country with the greatest potential for continuing emission-reducing improvements in energy efficiency. Indeed, in the first commitment period under the Kyoto Protocol it could be described as the Saudi Arabia of the emerging carbon market, with the potential to try to manipulate the market through strategic decisions as to when and how it releases its surplus – if there are buyers willing to deal.

But such trading is not an automatic right under the treaty; it requires

the institutions and information to match. Although Russia's forests are of global significance in relation to the carbon cycle, climate and the Kyoto Protocol, it is the energy sector that takes centre stage. Primary and secondary fossil fuels account for about 89% of Russia's total GHG emissions and over 97% of its CO_2 emissions.[2] Understanding Russia's view means understanding the central role of energy in Russia's economy. The energy industry accounts for over one-quarter of its GDP and over half of the federal budget, exports and hard currency earnings.[3] Always important, the share of oil and gas production in Russia's economy has grown in recent years and now approaches that of many OPEC countries.[4] In 2002, oil and natural gas exports made up 42% of total export income.[5] Yet the energy sector is in dire need of further reform and new investment, and for many Russians the Kyoto Protocol only makes sense if it contributes to that objective.

The issues raised are closely related to those surrounding foreign investment more generally. Historically Russia has had one of the lowest rates of foreign direct investment (FDI) among industrialized countries ('Annex B' countries in the Kyoto Protocol) that are classified as economies in transition (EITs). By April 2003, cumulative FDI in Russia since 1991 was just under US$20 billion. Currently only 13% of total investment into the energy sector originates from outside Russia, and of that 95% goes into the oil industry. There was practically no FDI into the electricity sector or other industries.[6] FDI made up only 5% of domestic fixed capital formation.[7] The growth in domestic investment (on average by some 10% per annum,[8] primarily powered by high fossil fuel prices on international markets) and some growth in FDI since 2003 have improved the rate of capital formation but much more is needed, given President Putin's goal of doubling GDP by 2010.

Russian decision-making is rarely easy to follow. This book lays out key features of past decision-making, and the present institutional responsibilities in relation to both the Kyoto mechanisms and future negotiations. It also explores past experience of international investment under the 'Activities Implemented Jointly' phase of the UN Framework Convention, and presents data on key Russian projects and potential.

Structure of the book

To cover such wide ground, the book is organized as follows. Chapters 2 and 3 assess the process of ratification, and the emission projections which have been a focus of debate over the economic pros and cons of ratification.

- Chapter 2 outlines Russia's past role in the international climate negotiations and the main factors driving the prolonged process of ratification of the Kyoto Protocol. In particular, it highlights that the final decision hinged less on environmental, or even economic, concerns than on internal and external politics – this has important implications for Russia's engagement in future international efforts to tackle climate change.
- Chapter 3 examines recent economic, energy and emission trends and future prospects for Russia's carbon dioxide emissions in the context of its Kyoto target and also of President Putin's goal to double Russia's gross domestic product (GDP) in ten years. Critically, the chapter concludes that under the most plausible growth scenarios, not only are Russia's emissions unlikely to exceed its Kyoto target but that the reforms required for rapid economic growth will also tend to accelerate energy efficiency improvements.

Chapters 4 to 7 assess the potential costs, benefits and opportunities surrounding Russian involvement in the Kyoto Protocol.

- Chapter 4 discusses Russia's opportunities in the emerging carbon markets. Many countries face significant challenges in achieving their Kyoto commitments and there are real opportunities for Russia to derive benefits from the treaty's 'flexibility mechanisms', international emissions trading and joint implementation. This chapter describes the mechanisms and related market developments and opportunities for Russia.
- Chapter 5 analyses the size of the surplus of emissions allowances which Russia will be entitled to sell under the Kyoto Protocol. It assesses the factors behind the value of the surplus, the influence on carbon prices and the likely value of the surplus under various growth, trade and market scenarios.

- Chapter 6 examines the potential impacts of international action on climate change on Russia's energy exports, and the effects on the competitiveness of its energy-intensive industries. The chapter considers the various impacts of differing levels of international participation in emissions trading.
- Chapter 7 looks at the prospects for – and value of – joint implementation in Russia. The chapter reviews the potential supply of and demand for projects in Russia, and the interest from potential international investors. Further, it focuses on various project types that are available and the value of such investments to Russia.

Chapters 8 to 10 assess the institutional realities and potential developments relating to the Kyoto Protocol in Russia.

- Chapter 8 looks back to the pilot phase of 'Activities Implemented Jointly' – emission reduction projects initiated in Russia under the terms of the Berlin Mandate before the Kyoto Protocol was agreed – and assesses which of the lessons learned remain relevant to future projects. The chapter also considers whether additional barriers have emerged since this pilot phase.
- Chapter 9 reviews the compliance requirements and options under the Kyoto Protocol. Compliance with institutional requirements, such as emission inventories and reporting, determines whether a country is entitled to participate in the Kyoto mechanisms. The chapter examines the issues surrounding Russian institutional compliance, and the implications of different levels of compliance for the mechanisms that could be utilized.
- Chapter 10 looks forward to Russian implementation of the Kyoto Protocol. Developments since ratification are reported with the main focus on the National Action Plan of the Russian government as presented in February 2005. The chapter then discusses the strategic option for Russia and prospects for effective implementation of the Protocol.

In conclusion, Chapter 11 brings together some of the core insights of the previous chapters in considering the potential and pitfalls, and the prospects and predictions, for future Russian involvement in addressing climate change.

2 THE ROAD TO RATIFICATION AND BEYOND

Introduction

Russia has emerged as a key player in the international climate regime. To come into force, the Kyoto Protocol required ratification by at least 55 countries, accounting for 55% of industrialized (Annex 1) country carbon dioxide emissions in 1990. While over 120 countries had ratified the Protocol by the autumn of 2004, these accounted for only 44% of Annex 1 emissions.[1] The withdrawal of the US from the Kyoto Protocol in March 2001 meant that Russia's assent was critical if it was to come into force.[2]

The road to Russian ratification was, however, protracted, tortuous and subject to heated internal – but very public – debate. To many in the West, this prevarication was puzzling as the widespread perception was that Russia had nothing to lose and everything to gain by the treaty's entry into force. However, Russia's approach to the issue was more complex and intrinsically bound up with the country's changing economic circumstances and internal political position, the economic importance of its energy sector and wider geopolitics.

This chapter traces the evolution of Russia's approach to the Kyoto Protocol, the pros and cons of ratification from a Russian perspective, and the internal and external forces at work. Finally, it looks forward to what this may mean for discussions on future negotiations on climate change. In doing so, the chapter draws both on published sources and on personal conversations with Russian and other international experts.[3]

Evolution of the Russian approach

Early marginal role

Russia was among the first to sign the UN Framework Convention on Climate Change (UNFCCC) during the UN Conference on Environment

and Development (UNCED) in Rio de Janeiro in 1992, and it ratified the Convention in 1994. Although some have argued that Russia was partly motivated by the potential negative effects of climate change,[4] its general approach to environmental treaties tended to be of a declarative nature and highly politicized, being dominated by foreign policy priorities.[5]

Russia played only a minor part in the early negotiations around the Convention, and its behaviour at the first Conference of Parties to the UNFCCC (COP-1) has been described as 'defensive and almost unnoticed'.[6] Its role consisted largely of lobbying for low commitments for economies in transition (EITs), opposing any strengthening of the Convention, assistance for joint implementation (JI), and the inclusion of forests as carbon sinks in the Kyoto regime.

At COP-2 in 1996, Russia appeared to be allied with the OPEC countries in obstructing strong international measures, owing to fears over the potential impact on energy export revenues.[7] It continued to express scepticism over the scientific findings of the Intergovernmental Panel on Climate Change (IPCC).[8]

Turning point – the Kyoto Protocol

The Kyoto Protocol marked a turning point in Russian climate policy. Although Russia continued to play a fairly passive role at COP-3 in Kyoto in December 1997, it nevertheless emerged as an important actor in the Kyoto process as a result of the laxity of its target and the intro-duction of the flexible mechanisms. At COP-3, Russia's approach was aligned with that of the JUSSCANNZ group,[9] which supported the concept of emissions trading and a multi-gas approach. It also became an advocate of the 'big bubble' idea which would allow Annex 1 countries to achieve their targets either individually or jointly.

In 1998, Russia became allied with the newly formed Umbrella Group[10] which furthered the goals of Russia, Ukraine and various OECD member countries outside the EU. The main focus of the group was to lobby for emissions trading without limits on its use. In short, the early Russian climate policy was a journey from reluctant participant to 'free marketeer' supporting ratification of the Kyoto Protocol.[11] Russia's active interest in the Kyoto Protocol stemmed from its success at negotiating a generous target for the first commitment period and potential revenues and investments under the Kyoto mechanisms.

At the time Kyoto was negotiated, Russia's emissions had fallen substantially as a result of the collapse of its industry in the early 1990s. It was understandably reluctant to sign up to any agreement that might constrain future growth, and it insisted on a right to return emissions to 1990 levels during the first commitment period. As a result, Russia is likely to be in a position of significant *over-compliance* with its emission limitation commitment and to sell its emissions surplus and attract investments through JI. As the head of the Russian delegation later explained, 'Naturally our attitude to this idea [emissions trading] was determined to a significant extent by the understanding whereby Russia could be one of

Table 2.1: Russian negotiating positions on the Kyoto mechanisms

Opposes	Supports
• Quantitative restrictions on the use of the Kyoto mechanisms • Supplementarity owing to negative effects on development of market • Qualification of Russia's emissions surplus as 'hot air' • Taxes on the implementation of the Kyoto mechanisms • Special status of CDM as it discriminates against JI and emissions trading	• Early start for emissions trading and JI • Banking and forward contracts • Flexible approach to compliance mechanisms, providing incentives rather than coercion or compulsion • High regulatory role for the state and government involvement • Forests as carbon sinks directly related to the Kyoto mechanisms • International support for capacity-building in EITs • Reinvestment of revenues from emissions trading into climate change mitigation projects

Source: Derived from Nikitina (2001), p. 206.

the large potential and prospective "sellers" of emissions quotas.'[12] Russia's main negotiating positions on the Kyoto mechanisms are summarized in Table 2.1. Many of these approaches were influenced by those of the US in the 1990s and have since been tightened or substantiated.

The lax targets and trading possibilities for Russia and other EITs were also an important factor in the United States' acceptance of a more stringent target for itself than many had expected, and early discussions involving Russia were focused on a US–Russia bulk deal on allowances.[13] Thus Russia's importance in international climate policy and its interests in it increased dramatically. Russia signed the Kyoto Protocol in March 1999.

Impact of the US withdrawal

The US withdrawal from the Kyoto process in 2001 critically influenced Russia's perceptions of its own interests. Not only did it leave Russia without a large potential purchaser of its emissions surplus, but carbon prices would be much lower owing to reduced demand. As Sergey Kuraev of the Russian Regional Ecological Centre observed, 'After the US withdrew from Kyoto, some influential Russian politicians started to say that Kyoto had lost its economic interest for Russia'.[14] (The impact of the US withdrawal on the value of Russia's surplus is discussed further in Chapter 5.)

More fundamentally, many Russian supporters of the Kyoto Protocol felt a sense of betrayal: they had been seduced into supporting the treaty on the basis of potential benefits they would now no longer receive.[15] By this time, too, the Russian economy was beginning to recover from the financial crisis of 1998. Not only did the potential revenues from Kyoto seem lower but the increase in emissions that accompanied economic growth gave rise to some concerns over whether Russia would have a surplus to sell. In addition, many Russians were very sceptical about whether there would be demand for Russia's emissions surplus from the EU, Japan and Canada. This was in part because of clear reservations on the part of the EU and others over buying what many saw as 'hot air', and in part because of potential competition from other EITs.

As a result, Russia's stance *vis-à-vis* Kyoto changed dramatically from supporter to somewhat unpredictable sceptic. More critically still for the Kyoto Protocol, the US withdrawal meant Russia became a much more important player in the international climate negotiations – a position it has used to its own great advantage. While the State Duma (Russia's

lower house of parliament) supported ratification in hearings organized in June 2001, the head of the Duma's Ecology Committee called for negotiations between Russia and the EU in order to 'set certain terms' prior to ratification. Thus in COP-6 Part II in July 2001, Russia declared that, provided the existing problems with the rules of the Protocol were resolved, it was ready to back the Bonn Agreement – a decision by Parties to the UNFCCC covering key outstanding issues on imple-mentation of the Kyoto Protocol and funding for developing countries, as required by the Buenos Aires Plan of Action, agreed by Parties in 1998. In COP-7 in Marrakech in November 2001, Russia demanded that the volume of carbon sinks allocated to the country under Article 3.4 should be doubled. Only when these demands were accommodated did Russia declare that it was ready to accept the Marrakech Accords.[16]

In all, Russia succeeded in using its role in the negotiations to great effect, securing concessions in a number of important areas. Meanwhile, the other big Kyoto players ratified one by one. Canadian ratification on 17 December 2002 left Russia in a decisive position with regard to the Protocol's entry into force. In subsequent COPs Russia has continued to press the case, in particular, for JI and its early application under less stringent criteria.

Progress towards ratification

Despite the disappointment of the US withdrawal, the Russian govern-ment remained generally positive on ratification in principle, although in discussions in April 2002 both the Russian cabinet and Putin himself called for an assessment of its pros and cons.[17] By June 2002, they had developed an action plan for the preparation of a decision on ratification. Hopes for an early decision were raised when at the World Summit for Sustainable Development in September 2002, Prime Minister Mikhail Kasyanov announced his belief that Russia would ratify in the near future.[18] In the same month, Alexander Kosarikov, deputy chair of the Duma's Ecology Committee, confirmed that the government planned to present the Protocol to the State Duma by the end of that year.[19] This was followed in October 2002 by a Statement of State Duma repre-sentatives in Delhi on the intention to ratify.

Even so, Putin's position remained ambiguous. While accepting that ratification did not carry any special risks for the country, he declared 'we

are not against it' – a comment that fell short of a clear intention to ratify.[20] Internationally, at a high-level Russia–UK energy conference held in London in June 2003, Russia presented itself as a country 'ready for business' along the lines of its Western counterparts but showed no interest in ratifying the Kyoto Protocol. Despite this, in the same month the working group of the Presidium of the State Council of the Russian Federation, chaired by President Putin, recommended ratification.[21] In July Russia's Economy Ministry declared that the Kyoto Protocol would not harm Russia's interest and that ratification was a political question awaiting a nod from the Kremlin.[22]

Another encouraging sign was that in September 2003, the Russian Interagency Committee on Climate Change approved a draft legal base for implementing the Kyoto Protocol prepared by the Ministry of Economy and an approach to JI proposed by Roshydromet. The following month, the Minister of Natural Resources Vitaly Artyukov initiated a pilot scheme for the Kyoto mechanisms in three regions in the Russian Federation.[23]

A positive decision for ratification also seemed to have a measure of internal support. According to Robert Nigmatullin, deputy chairman of the Duma's Ecology Committee, most Russian parliamentarians supported the Protocol.[24] A further promising sign, from a Western perspective, was the formation in July 2003 of the National Carbon Union (NCU) which aimed for both ratification of the Kyoto Protocol and its effective implementation.[25] The NCU includes major energy and industrial producers in Russia, which are significant emitters of greenhouse gases. RAO UES is the world's largest GHG emitter. Prior to this, industry had played a minor role in the discussions over the Kyoto Protocol, in part because of the traditional divide between politics and society.[26] Although RAO UES was active in the late 1990s it had previously withdrawn from the international arena.

Similarly encouraging was the fact that in June 2003, the Advisory State Council to the Kremlin – on which sit the governors of the country's 89 regions – called on Russia to ratify the treaty by September of that year.[27] Regional support and cooperation are not only crucial for implementation but the activities of the regions account for a significant share of GHG emissions. This said, while business and regional support for environmental regulation generally is seen as positive in the West, the situation is less clear cut in Russia, given Putin's drive to keep

industrialists out of politics and to attain greater control over the regions. Moreover, there is a potential conflict of regional and federal interests over property rights, which the federal government views as its prerogative, but which the regions feel belong to them.[28]

Even so, in the light of these developments, there were high hopes among some Western Kyoto advocates that Putin would use his hosting of the World Climate Change Conference (WCCC) in Moscow in September 2003 to announce a firm intention to ratify the Kyoto Protocol. In the event, they were to be disappointed. Not only did the conference hall echo to a chorus of scepticism over the reality and causes of climate change, but President Putin made it clear that the government was still studying the question. Critically, he also stated that the decision would be made 'in accordance with Russia's national interests'. He urged the international community not to put pressure on Russia to ratify.[29] Putin's identification of 'national interest' as the key criterion for decision marked a shift in Russia's approach to the issue. The decision was not simply one of climate policy but to be assessed at the higher level of economic, social and foreign policy.[30]

Prevarication and debate

The mood of scepticism at the WCCC was followed by months of intense – and very public – debate within Russia over the pros and cons of ratification, summarized in Table 2.2. This debate was reflected in conflicting – and increasingly negative – reports in the media. A typical example was a statement from Andrey Illarionov, Economic Adviser to the President, on 2 December 2003 that 'This protocol cannot be ratified', contradicted the next day by Mukhamed Tsikhanov, the Deputy Economy Minister: 'There are no decisions about ratification apart from the fact that we are moving towards ratification.'

By April 2004, Russia's political establishment appeared deeply divided on the Kyoto Protocol. At hearings on ratification in the State Duma there was strong opposition to the treaty, with three committees (Ecology, Economy and International Affairs) issuing a joint statement that ratifying Kyoto was 'inexpedient' and pointless in the light of the US decision to abandon the treaty and the non-participation of other major developing countries.[31] Meanwhile the Russian Industry and Economy Ministries (MIE and MEDT) urged Putin to ratify.[32]

Table 2.2: Arguments in Russia for and against ratification of the Kyoto Protocol (2002–4)

For	Against
• Climate change could have adverse impacts, particularly in vulnerable permafrost areas and through sea level rise in coastal zones.	• Extent of human-induced climate change is uncertain
• Sales of Russia's likely emissions surplus could bring in revenue.	• Climate change may be advantageous for Russia as it is a cold country
• JI would enhance foreign investment prospects.	• Costs of domestic implementation
• Investments under the Kyoto mechanisms could support modernization in the energy sector and help drive innovation.	• Revenues from the Kyoto mechanisms are likely to be low
• Improvements in energy efficiency are also critical to future economic growth.	• Post-2012 GHG limits could clash with Russia's economic growth ambitions
• Measures to reduce GHGs could also improve the domestic environment.	• The Kyoto Protocol is unfair as not all countries have taken on emissions commitments
• Ratification and implementation of the Kyoto Protocol may smooth the way for Russia's entry into the WTO.	• The Kyoto Protocol without the US, the largest economy in the world, is pointless
• Participation in the Kyoto Protocol would improve Russia's image in the global arena and demonstrate its support for multilateralism.	• The Kyoto Protocol is ineffective: something more radical is required

Source: Derived from Nikitina (2003), Pluzhnikov (2002) and Williamson (2004).

Much of the furore seems to have been fuelled by the activities of Professor Yuri Izrael, Director of the Institute of Global Climate and Ecology of Roshydromet and the Russian Academy of Sciences (RAS), and Andrey Illarionov. Much climate work in Russia is concentrated around Izrael, who is renowned for his scepticism over the causes of climate change and declarations that global warming would be beneficial to Russia. His influence was evident in the high profile given to sceptics at the WCCC, where in practice he chaired the organizing committee. Similarly he was undoubtedly influential in the decision by the RAS not to support ratification in May 2004.[33]

Russia's official position on the risks of climate change, as laid out in its National Communications to the UNFCCC, is more balanced. It recognizes the potential adverse effects of, for example, sea level rise on coastal regions and vulnerable permafrost areas. Even so, given that scientific views have a major influence on public opinion on climate change, Izrael's widely publicized remarks contributed to low levels of public support for the Kyoto Protocol. Although many educated Russians believed that climate change exists and could be a problem, they remained deeply sceptical about the role of human activities and, in any case, are suspicious of the Kyoto Protocol itself. It was typically viewed as a bureaucratic tool to sell Russian natural resources – clean air – and to compromise Russian sovereignty by giving up control over GHG emissions.[34] More generally, climate change as a long-term global problem remained a low priority relative to more immediate and pressing issues.

After the WCCC, it was Illarionov – arguably the most powerful of the Kyoto Protocol's critics in Russia – who stole the headlines. Putin's own lack of economic background means that on economic questions he relies heavily on others. Illarionov, having established his reputation as a commentator on economic policy during the Yeltsin years, was viewed as a credible source of independent advice on external economic affairs.[35] In a seemingly one-man international campaign against ratification, he argued that: the Protocol unfairly discriminated against Russia and would hamper economic growth; Russia would not be able to sell its surplus allowances and would ultimately be compelled to be a buyer rather than a seller of emissions; and in any case the Protocol was based on flawed science and would not achieve its own objectives.[36] He was also instrumental in stirring up debate in the April 2004 hearings in the Duma.

The appearance of intense debate around these issues in Russia led some to speculate that this might be the end of the road for the Kyoto Protocol. Increasingly, the question became not *when* Russia would ratify, but *whether* it intended to do so and, more particularly, *why* it was prevaricating. To many in the West, however, much of this debate seemed designed to raise the asking price for ratification. The ease with which the ratification bill eventually passed through the State Duma (see below) lends weight to this speculation.

A political decision

The intense debate in Russia distracts from the fact that the decision on ratification of the Kyoto Protocol was ultimately down to Putin. Russian federal law on international agreements requires the consent of both the Federal Assembly and the President. Within this process the President has a particularly decisive role. Before a draft law can be submitted to the State Duma it must be signed by the President or the Prime Minister or the latter's deputy on behalf of the Cabinet. Even if the law is passed, it cannot come into force without the President's signature.[37] Add to this the fact that not only did the parliamentary elections in December 2003 give control of the Duma and its committees to the pro-Kremlin United Russia party, but Putin's power was reinforced by his landslide victory in the presidential elections in March 2004, and the ratification decision was in his gift.

For Putin, the question of ratification was a political issue, rather than an environmental one or related to gains under the Kyoto mechanisms.[38] Putin's framing of the decision as a question of the country's 'national interest' highlighted the fact that environment is subordinate to higher economic and development priorities.[39] Nor was environment high on the public's agenda, compared with more immediate problems. Indeed in the recent elections, parties which focused on the environment got few votes.[40] To the extent that environment was an issue at all, it was the legacy of nuclear and chemical contamination from the Soviet era that was the concern.

While many outsiders pointed to the potential economic gains under the Kyoto Protocol, in reality this was not a big issue for Russia in view of the modest returns anticipated after the US withdrawal and particularly, given the revenues from high oil prices, reductions in external

debt and Russia's improved investment rating. Indeed, as Alexey Kokorin of WWF Russia observed in November 2003, for Putin Kyoto was a 100% political problem masked by economic concerns.[41]

Kyoto diplomacy

Key political considerations for Russia included both how to balance US and EU positions and how to win maximum political kudos from ratification. In line with his general approach to foreign policy, Putin used Russia's pivotal position to more general political advantage, initially seeking guarantees of income under the Kyoto mechanisms, but later looking for concessions on unrelated foreign policy issues.[42]

The US

There is little evidence that the US exerted direct pressure on Russia not to ratify the Kyoto Protocol, but this does not mean that it had no influence on Russia's decision. As mentioned earlier, the mere fact of the US withdrawal certainly reduced Russia's economic interests in the Kyoto Protocol, since it was left without a major potential buyer of its emissions surplus. In addition, some Russians questioned how a poor country like Russia could afford the treaty if a rich country like the US was concerned about its economic impact. This point ignores the two countries' very different positions under the Kyoto Protocol: the US would be obliged to take action to cut emissions, whereas Russia, in theory at least, could gain through sales of its surplus. However, the US position certainly gave ammunition to the sceptics.

Some observers also claim to have detected a change in Russia's stance on the Kyoto Protocol following a visit to Moscow by senior US climate negotiator Harlan Watson in January 2003.[43] As a result of this meeting, Russia and the US issued a joint statement agreeing to explore common approaches to climate change. They also formed a working group to facilitate this process, with a first meeting scheduled for the following April, and agreed to cooperate closely on preparations for the WCCC.[44] Part of the US intent in this may have been to emphasize the benefits of bilateral agreements as an alternative to multilateral agreements.[45]

A further factor in the US's favour was that it would almost certainly have been Russia's preferred partner on climate change. Not only does Russia regard the US as a significant partner in foreign policy but the US

has strong strategic energy and security interests in Russia. Russia also finds the US more straightforward to deal with than the EU. In addition, both the current US administration and Russia share a scepticism over the science of climate change and, in different ways, are in thrall to the energy industry. This said, Russia is at least theoretically committed to multilateral approaches to international problems (although in practice tending to be pragmatic, working with others when this is in its own interest and on conditions acceptable to itself[46]).

While Russia would not have wished to endanger relations with the US, it was unlikely that the relationship would be seriously damaged by Russian ratification of Kyoto if no other major issues were linked to this decision. Mutual cooperation on climate change did not ultimately stop Russia from ratifying, but it may have slowed down the process. Indeed, one effect seems to have been to raise the stakes required for Russian ratification, as Russia put pressure on the EU for greater technological collaboration and recognition of Russia as a privileged partner on energy and the environment.[47]

The EU

In contrast with the US, the EU overtly tried to influence Russia's decision on ratification. During 2003 and early 2004, Russia was faced with a succession of visits – and calls to ratify – from the Commission and EU member states.[48] Further pressure also came from outside, including UN Secretary General Kofi Annan.[49] Approaches to Russia in the run-up to the Moscow conference generally elicited positive responses, but afterwards both parties became increasingly frustrated with each other. The EU's irritation stemmed from both a genuine desire to see the Kyoto Protocol enter into force and, perhaps, a more immediate need to keep its own wavering member states in line. Russia, on the other hand, became increasingly irritated by the pressure from the EU and the lack of coordination of EU activities – Russia would much rather deal with a single representative than a multitude of member states.

The roots of this mutual frustration lay in a mismatch in expectations of the Kyoto Protocol. In general the EU's arguments focused on appeals to the global good, Russia's responsibility to participate in efforts to tackle an international problem, the opportunity to demonstrate commitment to multilateral efforts and to show leadership and participate in the Kyoto mechanisms. From the Russian perspective, not only was protection of the

global environment not a priority given its own economic situation. It was the EU and other Kyoto Parties that needed Russia, and needed the treaty to come into force, not the other way around, as it was clear that Russia was likely to meet its Kyoto emissions commitments domestically. Nor did the Russians see the fate of the Kyoto Protocol as dependent on them, given that some other countries (i.e. the US) had not ratified.[50]

What Russia wanted was tangible incentives from the EU (and Canada and Japan) in the form of 'guaranteed benefits' through bulk trades under the Kyoto Protocol.[51] However, as EU Environment Commissioner Margot Wallström noted, 'the quantity of emission credits to be traded or investments to be undertaken will be determined by the market'.[52] Russia had been similarly disappointed by the EU's response to its declaration that it would be willing to recycle revenues from international emissions trading into environmental projects under a Green Investment Scheme (GIS – see Chapter 4). This was intended to help allay international apprehensions about purchases of emissions surpluses with no environmental benefit, and Russia expected to receive offers for bulk deals from the EU. It was thus disappointed when the EU, despite acknowledging that this was a good idea, questioned how to put it into practice.

For its part, the EC offered €2 million to Russia in technical aid under the TACIS programme to help ratification. Russia viewed this as wholly inadequate; one Russian official suggested that Moscow was looking to Europe, Japan and Canada for no less than €3 billion a year invested in JI projects with Russian companies.[53] While the EU's offer was intended as a measure of good faith, Russia suspected even the concept of technical aid of being a hidden subsidy for donor-country businesses. Kokorin speculated at the time that any efforts to 'buy' ratification would not help and indeed could have a negative effect.[54]

A more deep-rooted problem was the general poor state of relations between the EU and Russia in early 2004. They had very different priorities and expectations over what they required of each other.[55] While Russia's priorities generally related to economic concerns such as entry into the WTO and securing markets for its oil and gas and access in an enlarged EU, the EU's priorities largely reflected social concerns over democracy, human rights and Russian support for the Kyoto Protocol. The importance of Russia's ratification to the EU was reflected in an assertion by French President Jacques Chirac, following Putin's speech at

the Moscow conference, that future EU–Russia relations depended on it.[56] In contrast, in February 2004, Russia asserted that the Kyoto Protocol would not determine relations between the two countries.[57] In the event, it was precisely these different priorities that provided the opportunity to secure Russian ratification.

The endgame

Political horse-trading

Most commentators agree that the deadlock was finally broken during a series of meetings between Russian and EU officials in the lead-up to a high-level EU–Russia summit in Moscow on 21 May 2004. During this period, both parties seemed to reach an understanding that if the EU supported Russia's early entry into the WTO then Putin would speed up examination of the ratification issue.

An early report of a connection between progress on the WTO and the Kyoto Protocol came in September 2003 when Duma members told visiting EU Members of Parliament that they would like to see more efforts from the EU before Russian ratification, notably with regard to Russia's entry into the WTO.[58] Russia has been seeking WTO entry since the early 1990s, but negotiations with the EU had stalled over Gazprom's gas export monopoly and the big difference in prices for domestic and foreign consumers. The EU's support is crucial to Russia as it is one of the most important power brokers in the WTO and Russia's main trading partner.[59]

While in the past the EU has argued that 'politics cannot shortcut economics',[60] in January 2004 the EU hinted at a possible trade-off between Russian ratification of the Kyoto Protocol and the EU easing Russia's path into the WTO.[61] This sort of political horse-trading of lower-priority issues for higher-priority ones is fairly standard within diplomatic circles. Rather than going for a straight trade-off, the EU argued that the Russian gas price reforms required for WTO accession implied the need for foreign investment to help Russian industry adapt – investment which would be best assured if linked to the Kyoto mechanisms.[62]

Terms for Russia's entry into the WTO were agreed at the EU–Russia summit in May 2004. In the wake of the summit, both Russian

and EU officials denied a direct link between this and Russia's ratification of the Kyoto Protocol. Indeed, Putin insisted that 'We do not tie up the WTO and the Kyoto Protocol.'[63] Certainly, the summit documents did not formally oblige Russia to ratify the Kyoto Protocol despite pressure from the EU that they should.

Nevertheless, some form of understanding was clearly reached. As Putin stated afterwards, 'The fact that the European Union has made concessions in our WTO negotiations cannot but have a positive effect on Moscow's attitude towards ratification of the Kyoto Protocol.'[64] In particular, he indicated that the agreement over the WTO 'reduced the risks for our economy in the mid-term prospect, and to a certain extent contributes to a faster resolution of the problem of Russia's joining the Kyoto Protocol.'[65] He went on to promise to accelerate the ratification process. Even so, he cautioned that Russia still had 'several concerns' about its obligations under the treaty and declined to set a firm date, saying this was a matter for parliament.

Russian ratification

Russia finally ratified the Kyoto Protocol in the autumn of 2004, going through the parliamentary process with little argument and in near record time. On 30 September, the government approved the Protocol and submitted it to the State Duma. On 22 October the Duma voted overwhelmingly to ratify the Protocol by a vote of 334 to 74.[66] The upper house endorsed the decision five days later and on 5 November the Kremlin announced that Putin had signed off the treaty. Despite the landmark status of the treaty, there was no fanfare, just a brief statement to the press. The last step was purely technical – Russia's submission of its ratification documents to the United Nations.

There are a number of possible explanations for the precise timing of the ratification decision.[67] While Putin certainly now had a motive to press forward with ratification – Russia's entry into the WTO – there was no deadline. A further incentive may have been that it seemed like a case of 'now or never' if Russia was to gain from the emerging carbon markets. One reason for the delay could have been that the government discussions on ratification that were necessary before a draft law could be introduced to the Duma were put back by three months from 20 May 2004 at the request of the Ministry of Economic Development and Trade (MEDT) – possibly because of the negative conclusion of the

RAS.[68] Alternatively, having extracted the required concessions, Putin may have delayed so as not to appear to be too close to the EU.

Russia's ratification was welcomed by the EU, Canada and Japan, with German Environment Minister Jürgen Tritten calling it 'evidence that Russia is aware of its responsibility in the battle with climate change'.[69] Illarionov's response was that the decision to ratify was 'very, very smart' as it kept Russia in good grace with the EU, which holds the keys to the country's economic development, while helping avoid the taint of unilateralism that haunts the US. Even so, he suggested that the lack of gains from the Kyoto Protocol would be so obvious to Russia, the EU and Japan that they would decide to do something more reasonable.[70] In any case, the ratification decision marks a significant stage in Russia's approach to climate change, although the political basis for the final decision raises serious questions over future policy.

Prospects for future negotiations

There is some evidence that, having established itself as a key player in the international climate regime, Russia intends to continue active engagement. As early as October 2004, Deputy Prime Minister Alexander Zhukov indicated that the following year Russia intended to begin negotiations with other Parties to the Protocol on the conditions for participation in its implementation from 2012.[71] Moreover, following the UK's initiative during its presidency of the G8 in 2005 to prioritize climate change, Russia has committed to keeping the issue on the agenda during its own G8 presidency in 2006. At the international climate negotiations (COP-11 and COP/MOP-1) in late 2005, Russia also agreed to future talks on both long-term cooperation under the UNFCCC and post-2012 commitments under the Kyoto Protocol.

Beneath this veneer of engagement, there remain reasons to be sceptical as to whether Russia will be a positive force in negotiations over future commitments. At COP/MOP-1 environmental NGOs accused Russia of stalling negotiations on future commitments through the introduction of irrelevant texts. In the G8 context, the climate issue is part of a wider agenda including energy security which, from a producer's perspective, means guaranteeing markets and high prices. While Russia certainly recognizes the need to diversify its economy and the importance of energy efficiency, energy exports remain critical to its

economic growth ambitions.[72] Thus Russia's stance in the climate negotiations is likely to remain closely linked to strategic interests in the energy sector. Similarly, ongoing concern over the interplay of emissions and the country's economic growth ambitions is likely to remain a key issue (see Chapter 3).

It cannot be presumed that because Russia has ratified the Kyoto Protocol, it will side with the EU in future negotiations. Russia has ongoing dialogues with both the EU and the US, accepting support from the former to assist in implementation of the Kyoto Protocol and from the latter for Arctic research.[73] Indeed, in some respects, Russia's interests seem closer to those of the US, given the prevailing mood of scientific scepticism, concern over economic impacts and interest in technological cooperation and investment.[74] Moreover, while the EU and Russia concluded bilateral negotiations on the latter's entry into the WTO in 2004, negotiations at a multilateral level were still ongoing in late 2005. If these do not progress satisfactorily from Russia's perspective, it may feel less inclined to follow through on the Kyoto Proocol.

A further open question is whether there is the political will to engage in further international climate agreements. The decision on the Kyoto Protocol was undoubtedly driven by Putin, but his term of office ends in 2008 and under the current constitution he cannot stand for re-election. Certainly, the ratification decision has done little to quieten Kyoto critics in Russia. Throughout 2005, Illarionov continued to argue against restrictions on greenhouse gas emissions on economic grounds – although his influence may be diminished following his resignation in December 2005.[75] Similarly, Izrael continues to try to undermine Russia's more progressive stance through reiteration of doubts over the link between human activity and global warming and the efficacy of the Kyoto Protocol,[76] and in summer 2005 a group of Russian scientists called on the president of the RAS to withdraw his signature from an international statement on climate change initiated by the Royal Society in the UK.[77]

Despite Russia's recent strong growth, economic and local environmental problems are likely to remain a higher priority than protecting the global environment – although this may change as the impacts of climate change become more apparent.[78] Indeed, while some areas may indeed benefit through extended growing or shipping seasons or reduced heating costs, the thawing of permafrost is already aggravating damage to buildings, airfields and pipelines in Siberia. In similarly positioned Alaska,

the yearly cost of damage to infrastructure due to warming has been estimated at US$35 million or 1.4 per cent of the total state budget. Costs to the Russian economy could be much higher given the large number of settlements, industry and oil and gas activity in permafrost regions.[79]

Under such circumstances, Russian support for and participation in international agreements on climate change cannot be assured. Indeed, there is no guarantee that Russia will even stick with the Kyoto Protocol (any Party may withdraw from the treaty three years after the date it entered into force).[80] To the extent that Russian climate policy is guided by current political circumstances, then as circumstances change so might Russia's position.

Conclusions

Russia's ratification was critical to bringing the Kyoto Protocol into force on 16 February 2005, but this landmark decision had more to do with political benefits than protection of the global environment or, given the withdrawal of the US, direct economic benefits. Putin has played Russia's pivotal position on the Kyoto Protocol to great tactical advantage both in the climate negotiations themselves and in securing concessions in unrelated policy areas.

In negotiations over future commitments, Russia will remain an important player not least because it is responsible for over 17% of Annex 1 (1990) emissions of carbon dioxide and because of the huge potential to reduce emissions through improvements in energy efficiency (see Chapter 3). On the face of it there is some scope for optimism in Putin's willingness to put climate change on the G8 agenda during Russia's presidency of that body and support for future talks on further commitments and cooperation in the international climate negotiations. However, under Putin Russian climate policy is likely to remain closely tied to wider national interests, and to a large extent Russia's engagement with international efforts to tackle climate change is likely to hinge on synergies with wider social, economic and political priorities. This, in turn, will be partly contingent on the effectiveness of implementation of the Kyoto Protocol in Russia (see Chapter 10), and on whether the Protocol delivers the benefits Russia hopes for.

3 RUSSIAN ENERGY AND CARBON DIOXIDE EMISSION PROSPECTS

A key issue for Russia is whether meeting its Kyoto target is compatible with future economic growth prospects and, in particular, with President Putin's declared goal to double Russia's gross domestic product (GDP) within ten years. As highlighted in Chapter 1, energy is one of the most important sectors in Russia's economy and policy-makers are inevitably cautious about any measures that may interfere with its development. This chapter examines recent economic, energy and emission trends and future prospects for Russia's carbon dioxide emissions in the context of the country's Kyoto target.

Recent trends

Russia's allocation under the Kyoto Protocol was by most standards generous and allows Russia to return its emissions to 1990 levels. This was later supplemented by an allowance of 33 million tonnes of carbon (MtC) of credits for absorption from its forests. Russia's emissions in 1999 (the most recent year of full inventory reported to the UNFCCC) were 38% below 1990 levels. So they can rise 60% from this level before breaching the Kyoto ceiling; Russia's allowance for managed forest credits adds an additional 5% headroom.[1]

Figure 3.1 shows Russia's GDP, energy consumption and carbon dioxide emission trends.[2] The sharp fall in economic activity of nearly 40% from 1990 to 1998 was accompanied by similar but smaller declines in energy consumption and carbon dioxide emissions of 36% and 30% respectively. As a result the energy and carbon intensities of the economy increased. With Russia's economic recovery, energy use and emissions also rose, but more slowly than GDP. While GDP grew by nearly 30% from 1998 to 2003, the energy and carbon intensities of the economy actually fell by close to 20%. By 2003, Russia's GDP was about 83% of

Figure 3.1: Development of Russia's GDP energy consumption and carbon dioxide emissions, 1990–2003 (% of 1990 levels)

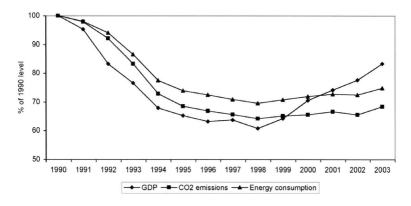

Source: The Institute of Energy Investigation of the Russian Academy of Sciences, Moscow.

1990 levels, while the corresponding figures for energy consumption and emissions were only about 75% and 68% respectively. The partial decoupling of GDP and carbon emissions since 1998 has important implications for projections of future emissions as it shows that growth need not be accompanied by a commensurate increase in pollution, Moreover, as this chapter demonstrates, Russia's emissions are unlikely to reach 1990 levels by the end of the first Kyoto commitment period.

Economic and energy developments

Forecasting economic and energy developments in a country undergoing total economic transformation is difficult. The turbulent economic history since 1990 removes any reliable base from which to extrapolate conditions within the economy and the recent (relative) political stability and legislative reforms are still too fragile to add any degree of certainty to future development.

The centrality of energy to the economy means that the Russian Energy Strategy (RES) is regularly updated. The Strategy sets forth the

main aims and lines of Russia's energy policy over the period to 2020 and plays an important part in informing Russian economic policy. The strategic goals of Russia's policy are energy security, energy efficiency,

Figure 3.2: GDP scenarios to 2020 for Russia

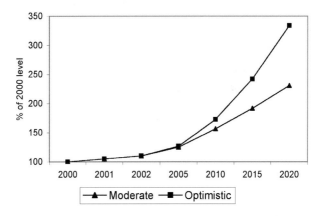

Figure 3.3: Energy intensity scenarios to 2020 for Russia

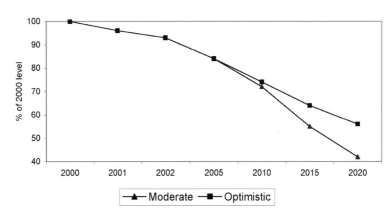

Source: RES (2003).

budgetary efficiency and environmental safety in the power sector. It is anticipated that achieving these goals will involve substantial reform of the energy sector, the first phase of which is due to be completed by 2010. More comprehensive reforms are anticipated later on.

The most recent Russian Energy Strategy gives a detailed presentation of assumptions and analysis of possible scenarios over the period to 2020.[3] Two of these scenarios are presented in Figures 3.2 and 3.3, which show that between 2000 and 2020, GDP could triple in the high case (termed the 'optimistic' variant in the Strategy) and more than double in the moderate case. The energy intensity of the economy (i.e. energy consumption per unit of GDP) over the same period is set to fall rapidly – to 42% and to 56% of their 2000 levels in the optimistic and moderate cases, respectively.

Realization of any particular scenario will hinge critically on the extent of reforms in the energy sector, a key part of which will be to improve energy efficiency. The following sections discuss the prospects for economic growth, energy intensity and carbon intensity under the Russian Energy Strategy and the impact of reform.[4]

Economic growth

A key determinant of future growth prospects is the extent to which economic reform measures will continue to be implemented. These include:

- Continued improvement to corporate governance in order to facilitate foreign investment.
- Reforms of Russia's economy in general and reform of the energy sector in particular. These include liberalization of energy prices on the domestic market, the breaking up of monopoly structures and the reduction or removal of energy subsidies.
- Incentives for growth in fixed capital formation, essential for greater energy efficiency in Russian industries.
- Structural reform of the economy with a shift from heavy, energy-intensive industries to service industries.
- International political and trade relations, in particular economic relations with the EU and the US, the terms of Russia's accession to the WTO, liberalization of international energy markets, etc.

The implementation of reform measures and their effectiveness are by no means certain. For example, plans to reform the electricity sector have existed for many years but have yet to be fully implemented, so prospects for current proposals remain unclear. Moreover, economic growth prospects will be contingent on both oil prices and improvements in energy efficiency.

The RES projects economic growth over the period to 2020 of between 2.7 and 6.2% per year, with a moderate annual growth scenario of 4.3%. These growth rates are somewhat lower than the sustained growth of 7.2% per year required to meet President Putin's objective of doubling Russia's GDP within ten years. The moderate projection is consistent with other recent projections by international agencies. In the *World Energy Outlook 2004,* the International Energy Agency (IEA) projects Russia's economic growth rates at between 3.4% and 4.4% over the period to 2020.[5] Similarly, the World Bank expects growth over the next few years of around 4–5% annually, but with little certainty of longer-term growth trends.

Higher estimates are seen by most Western commentators as optimistic, despite Russia's recent strong growth rates, which averaged 6.5% during the period 1999–2003 (OECD 2004). This growth has been fuelled by the escalation of oil prices from around US$10 a barrel in the late 1990s to over US$60 a barrel by August 2005. Analysis by the World Bank of the impact of oil prices on Russia's GDP growth shows that in the past GDP growth rates of more than 4–5% have only been realized when the oil price rose significantly during the year.[6] Although the impact of oil price on growth can be overstated, the OECD has calculated that, had oil prices remained stable over the recent period, this would have shaved an average of 1.6% off Russia's economic growth.[7]

This implies that achieving a 6.2% growth per year (let alone the 7.2% political target) on a sustainable basis could require oil prices to continue to rise on the international markets. While prices remain very volatile and future spikes are probable, repeated price hikes are unlikely to be sustainable in the long run. Indeed, the cyclical nature of the oil price market means that, if anything, average prices could fall over the decade to 2015.[8]

In the absence of major oil price rises, high levels of economic growth could only be achieved by exceptionally effective and rapid implementation of reforms across the whole economy, further rises in productivity

levels and reductions in energy intensity. While general conditions exist for these reforms to be implemented – buoyant economy, considerable cash reserves and a legislative chamber that closely toes Putin's policy line – the recent pace of change has not been fast enough.[9]

Igor Bashmakov of CENEf (the Centre for Energy Efficiency) argues that Russia will not be able to meet its ambitious growth targets without significant improvements in energy efficiency. Energy export revenues are likely not only to remain critical to Russia's economic growth over the period to 2010 and beyond, but to act as a 'pull' on growth in other sectors. Bashmakov further argues that if Russia doubles its GDP with present energy intensity levels, it would lose its capacity to export oil and gas by 2010.[10] Maintaining 2002 oil and gas export levels while doubling GDP would require an annual energy productivity growth of 4.8%. If Russia is only able to sustain the rates achieved by energy productivity improvements in 2000–03 (2.3%), then GDP could only grow by 50–70% of its 2001 level between 2002 and 2010. Thus Bashmakov concludes that while Russia needs an *effective* energy efficiency policy to reach its Kyoto target, it needs a *revolutionary* efficiency policy to double GDP by 2010.

Energy intensity

The Russian Energy Strategy recognizes that future economic growth is likely to increase energy demand but also highlights the paramount importance of improving energy efficiency in order to sustain economic growth. Together with other transition countries of central and eastern Europe, Russia has historically had one of the most energy-intensive economies in the world. The levels of energy intensity have been 2.3 times greater than the global average and up to 3.1 times the average level in the EU.[11]

Such comparisons need to be treated with caution for reasons concerned with both data compatibility and Russia's geography, climate and industrial structure. Russia is a very large country with a very harsh climate, and energy for heat is critical for survival. About 30% of the population live in areas where January temperatures range between −15° and −40°C and large communities exist in the permafrost areas which make up 59% of the territory. Russia's economy has also traditionally been heavily weighted towards industrial processes that consume large quantities of energy. Such factors account for part of the difference

between Russia's energy intensity and those of OECD countries. Nevertheless, Canada is a similarly sparse, cold and resource-intensive country, but figures from the Russian Ministry of Energy show that in 2000 Russia's energy intensity (PPP corrected) was 77% higher than that of Canada.[12]

Such international comparisons suggest the potential for big improvements in energy intensity but, as discussed above, the extent to which these are realized is likely to depend significantly on economic reforms, particularly in the energy sector. Energy intensity levels in Russia's economy fell by 11% over the period 1992–2002 but this resulted primarily from a decline in heavy industry and does not reflect improvements in the technical efficiency of energy equipment and appliances.[13] Indeed, energy intensity levels remain significantly higher than in other countries.

Future rates of reduction in energy intensity will be determined by the pace and degree of reforms in the energy sector as well as the related level of investment. If, and as, market reforms are implemented and economic structures change, there are indeed persuasive arguments to suggest that Russia's energy intensity could fall further and faster than assumed in the

Figure 3.4: Projected impact of economic reform and technical energy saving on energy consumption growth (mtoe)

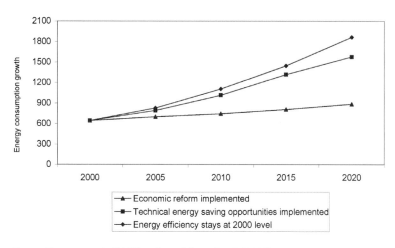

Source: Tangen et al. (2002), adapted from RES (2003).

RES. The centrally planned economy of the Soviet Union was one of the least energy-efficient in the world. While much progress has been made since 1992, market reform in the gas and electricity industries has been slower than in many other parts of the economy. This is the main reason why the Strategy shows (Figure 3.4) that economic reform will lead to only a marginal increase in energy demand by 2020; it also shows that if energy intensity were to remain at the 2000 level, energy demand would increase in line with economic growth.

How and why might such improvements occur? One of the hallmarks of the Soviet economy was the very slow turnover of capital stock. This means that Russia's economy, even in its current state of transition, is still saddled with many industries using extremely energy-inefficient plants and equipment which are many decades old. The intended take-off of capital investment, particularly post-2010 (see Figure 3.5), will be one of the most important drivers of energy efficiency as it will inevitably be associated with far more modern technology and management practices.

Combining the GDP and energy intensity scenarios from Figures 3.2 and 3.3 with the projected impact of economic reform in Figure 3.4 suggests that economic growth will be associated with improvements in energy efficiency and a fall in energy intensity. This is counter-intuitive for some Russian observers who tend to believe, in line with the conventional wisdom in the OECD in the 1970s, that increased economic

Figure 3.5: Level of capital investment to 2020

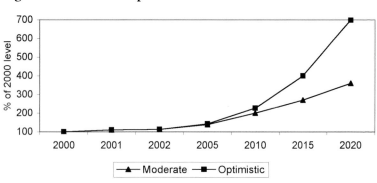

growth requires a roughly equivalent increase in energy use. For Russia in particular, starting as it does from such a low base in terms of energy efficiency, the opposite is likely to be the case. This is because the reforms required to achieve higher levels of economic growth will necessarily involve a high turnover of capital stock and retirement of inefficient plants. Moreover, structural changes from heavy industry towards light industry and services will result in reduced energy intensity.

The result of this process is likely to be, at least in the early years, a decline in the energy intensity of the economy. By contrast, a lack of market reform and slow economic growth is the scenario most likely to lead to increasing energy demand.

Other central and east European economies have managed to grow since 1995 without emitting more carbon per unit of output, and some have reduced absolute emission levels. Figure 3.6 shows the growth rate of emissions per capita versus income per capita in some economies in transition. Azerbaijan, Belarus, the Baltic states and Kazakhstan all experienced economic growth rates per capita of above 4% even as carbon emissions fell. Even in countries where emissions have increased, such as Armenia, Croatia and Slovenia, the rate of increase has been much less than that in GDP. Owing to the short time span, it is unlikely that the

Figure 3.6: Per capita GDP growth rates versus per capita carbon growth rates, 1995–2001

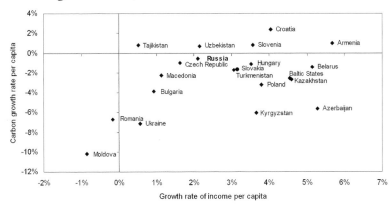

Source: M. Grubb, L. Butler and O. Feldman, 'Analysis of the relationship between growth in carbon dioxide emissions and growth in income', Working Paper, Faculty of Applied Economics, Cambridge University, 2006, *www.econ.cam.ac.uk.*

low growth rates for carbon emissions are in any major way influenced by reductions in the carbon intensity of fuels used (switching electricity generation from coal to gas, for example, is likely to take much longer than five years). Assuming then that for most countries the carbon intensity levels are generally stable over this period, GDP growth rates of 4% with no change in the growth of carbon emissions imply a comparable rate of reduction in energy intensity.

Carbon intensity

The future carbon intensity of energy consumption depends upon the expected evolution of the fuel and energy balance in the economy. In comparison to some of the other central and east European countries, Russia's energy sector has a relatively low carbon intensity level. However, according to a study by Fankhauser and Lavric (2003a), Russia's fuel- switching potential (i.e. switching from carbon-intensive fuels such as coal to those with lower carbon emissions such as natural gas) is also relatively low, primarily because natural gas already forms about 50% of its current fuel mix. In addition non-fossil fuels, mainly nuclear, form about 9%. In 1998 Russia's fuel mix was only 10–15% more carbon-intensive than the EU average, compared with Romania (106%) and Poland and Bulgaria (around 30%).

Table 3.1: Projected evolution of Russia's fuel mix and implications for carbon intensity (base year 2000)

Growth in carbon intensity	Reduction in carbon intensity
• Decline of natural gas in the fuel mix from 50% to 49% in 2010 and 46% in 2020. • Rise in coal production and usage from 19% to about 20% in 2020. • Rise in the use of oil and its derivatives from 20% to 22% in 2020.	• Increase in hydro and nuclear power generation within the fuel mix from 10.8% to 12% in 2020. • Modest increase in the use of renewable energy, especially in regions furthest from the centre.

Source: CEPA (2004), based on RES (2003).

In the Russian Energy Strategy, only a limited change to the carbon intensity of energy generation is envisaged by 2020, as a modest rise in the use of nuclear renewable energy sources and nuclear is offset by a planned switch from gas to coal (see Table 3.1). This may be over-pessimistic. While the Strategy reiterates a long-standing intention to switch some energy sources in European Russia from gas to coal, the price projections and the capital and lead-time requirements for coal plants make it hard to see this happening on a scale that would fundamentally change the emission projections discussed here.[14] Experience from OECD countries also suggests that, once the switch to gas has been made – particularly in power generation – a country is unlikely to return to large-scale coal use.

Implications for future carbon dioxide emissions

Official projections

Russia's Third National Communication to the UNFCCC presents three scenarios for energy and emission trends to 2020 based on the General Provisions of the Russian Energy Strategy (2000).[15] Under all three scenarios, carbon dioxide emissions are projected to remain below 1990 levels throughout the first Kyoto commitment period, ranging from 76% to 93% of 1990 levels in 2012 (see Table 3.2).

Table 3.2: Projections of CO_2 emissions (1990 = 100%)

Year	Scenario I	Scenario II	Scenario III
1990	100.0	100.0	100.0
2000	69.2	69.2	69.2
2005	74.6	72.0	78.4
2008	**78.0**	**73.8**	**84.5**
2010	**80.4**	**75.0**	**88.9**
2012	**82.8**	**76.2**	**93.4**
2015	86.7	78.0	100.7
2020	93.4	81.2	114.1

Source: NC3 (2002).

Note: **bold figures** shows Kyoto first commitment period.

The IEA's reference scenario in *World Energy Outlook 2004* suggests that emissions could be still lower than suggested by the official projections, being just 72% of their 1990 levels during the period 2008–12 and 11% lower than 1990 levels in 2030.[16] Under an Alternative Policy Scenario with accelerated energy efficiency improvements, the IEA suggests that emissions in 2030 could be 17% lower than 1990 levels in 2030.

Alternative scenarios

To explore the implications for carbon dioxide emissions for a wider range of possible futures, CEPA (2004) have projected carbon emissions over the next 20 years for a number of scenarios of economic growth and energy intensity reductions.[17] The model they use[18] is very similar to that used by the Russian government in its Third National Communication to the UNFCCC. Given the importance of reform in determining future developments in the energy sector and the links between economic growth and energy intensity, CEPA present two groups of scenarios:

- **Reform scenarios.** These assume reforms take place, resulting in rapid growth and significant improvements in energy intensity.
- **Non-reform scenarios.** These assume little or no reform, resulting in sluggish growth and little or no improvement in energy intensity.

A summary of the GDP growth and energy intensity assumptions used in their scenarios is set out in Table 3.3 and compared with the growth assumptions in the Russian Energy Strategy. Both sets of scenarios assume no change in carbon intensity (in line with the Russian government's own projections).

Of the growth rates assumed under the *reform scenarios*, three are similar to those in the Russian Energy Strategy. The 6% scenario requires both significant reform and rising fossil fuel prices, while the 2% scenario implies either less effective reform measures and/or declining fossil fuel prices. The moderate growth (4%) scenario is also roughly in line with the IEA and World Bank projections. Putin's challenge of doubling GDP by 2010 is reflected in the highest growth scenario of 7.2%.

The *non-reform scenarios* consider the possibility of economic stagnation to a maximum growth rate of 4%. The more optimistic scenario

Table 3.3: Energy intensity and economic scenarios used for emissions projections

(a) Energy intensity reduction per year (%)

Scenario	High reductions	Low reductions
Reform	4	2
Non-reform	2	0

(b) GDP growth per year (%)

Scenario	Optimistic	Moderate	Critical	Putin's challenge
Reform	6	4	2	7.2
Non-reform	4	2	0	N/A
Russian Energy Strategy	6.2	4.3	2.7	N/A

Source: CEPA (2004).

assumes that, even without significant reform or investment, some growth could still occur through more efficient use of existing capital equipment and the effects of increasing fossil fuel prices.

Figure 3.7 shows the energy-intensity reduction assumptions used in the CEPA scenarios relative to past changes in energy intensity. The greater rates of energy efficiency improvement assumed are consistent with experience from other transition economies and Russia's declared objective to reform and improve efficiency (see earlier discussion). In the absence of reform, it is still plausible that some modest improvements in energy intensity will occur and thus energy intensity projections are of 0% and 2% p.a.

Together, these scenarios represent a wider range of possible economic and energy futures than Russian official projections. Given the ongoing transformations in Russia, it is difficult to ascribe a relative likelihood to each of the scenarios. But recent experience, together with Russia's declared ambitions and ongoing reform programme, suggest that the medium- to higher-growth scenarios with modest improvements in energy efficiency are probably the most plausible. In the light of

Figure 3.7: Past and projected changes in energy intensity

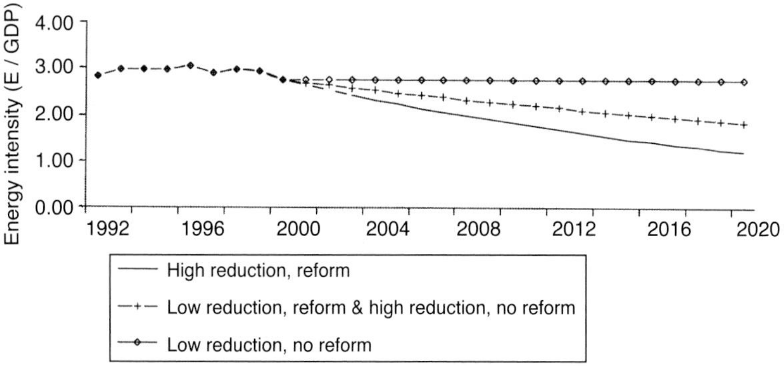

Source: CEPA (2004).

the earlier discussion of the dependency of growth on improvements in energy efficiency, the scenarios showing 7.2% GDP growth with 2% reduction in energy intensity, and 4% GDP growth with no change in energy intensity seem highly unlikely. The level of energy waste implied by no or little improvement in energy efficiency and the consequent loss of export potential could itself be a significant constraint on Russia's economic growth.

The implications of the various *reform* and *non-reform scenarios* for carbon dioxide emissions are shown in the four diagrams in Figure 3.8. These reflect the model assumption that the level of carbon dioxide emissions relates directly to economic growth, after taking into account anticipated reductions in energy intensity and carbon intensity of energy used. A key finding is that under all the scenarios, Russia would meet its Kyoto target. In 12 of the 14 scenarios, Russia's emissions remain below 1990 levels throughout the first commitment period. Two of the scenarios do suggest that Russia's emissions could exceed 1990 levels by 2012, but this potential 'shortfall' in the final couple of years is offset by the surplus available in 2008–10. Moreover, if Russia's carbon sink allocation is also taken into account, net emissions would almost certainly stay below Russia's Kyoto target.

Looking forward, the scenarios do raise other important issues with respect to post-2012 commitments. Encouragingly, most plausible

Figure 3.8: Projected CO_2 emissions under various economic and energy intensity scenarios

a) Reform scenarios

4% energy intensity reduction p.a.   2% energy intensity reduction p.a.

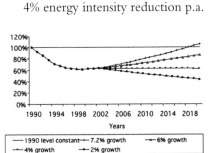

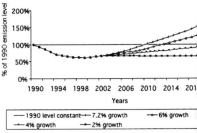

b) Non-reform scenarios

2% energy intensity reduction p.a.   0% energy intensity reduction p.a.

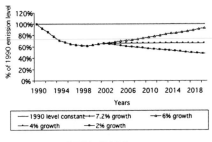

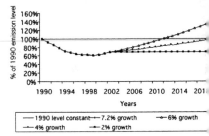

Source: CEPA (2004).

scenarios suggest that Russia's emissions are likely to remain below 1990 levels until at least 2020. However, in the highly unlikely event that higher growth were achieved with minimal improvements in energy efficiency, then emissions could be some 50% or more above 1990 levels by 2020. Similar projections have caused some to raise concerns that Kyoto could thus become a 'cross' (or burden) for Russia's back.[19]

Unsurprisingly, the question of future emissions continues to be a key issue for Russian policy-makers. In mid-2005, the government issued a tender for three studies which will examine Russia's greenhouse gas emissions to 2012 and 2020 (and optimal implementation of the Kyoto

mechanisms).[20] The conclusion is expected to influence Russia's position on a post–2012 regime. However, it is important to note that the existing target relates only to the 2008–12 period and all commitments post-2012 remain to be negotiated. Russia secured a good deal in Kyoto's first round of commitments, and there is no reason why it should not secure a reasonable deal in subsequent rounds. More fundamentally, technology studies show huge potential for continuing increases in efficient and low-carbon-emitting technologies. Thus future emissions are to a large extent in Russia's hands.

Conclusions

The above analysis finds that despite the recent upturn in Russia's carbon dioxide emissions, they are highly unlikely to exceed the country's current Kyoto target and indeed could well stay below 1990 levels until 2020. This is because sustainable economic growth and improvements in energy intensity are intrinsically – and inversely – linked. For Russia to meet its ambitious growth objectives, significant improvement in energy intensity will be necessary. International comparisons of both absolute energy intensities and the trend of emissions in other transition economies indicate that the economic reforms sought in Russia to underpin rapid economic growth would also lead to rapid declines in energy and associated emissions intensities. This combination suggests that scenarios in which Russia's emissions grow substantially in a decade, even by 60% or more, are not credible. Indeed the economic burden of wasting so much energy would be an impediment, not a corollary, to rapid economic development.

4 RUSSIAN OPPORTUNITIES IN THE KYOTO MARKET

As discussed in Chapter 3, under the most plausible growth scenarios, Russia's emissions are highly unlikely to exceed its Kyoto target. Other countries face a much more significant challenge in achieving their commitments and are likely to seek to use international flexibility mechanisms established under Kyoto to lower their compliance costs. These mechanisms have the effect of putting a price on carbon and enable countries to seek out cost-effective reductions in emissions. The real opportunities for Russia derive from the use of these mechanisms which allow trading of national emissions allowances and credits for investments through joint projects resulting in emissions reductions.

This chapter describes the mechanisms established under Kyoto and related market developments and the opportunities these present for Russia. The size and value of these potential opportunities are discussed in following chapters.

Kyoto mechanisms

The Kyoto Protocol establishes three international mechanisms to help Annex B countries (those taking on emissions caps) to meet their targets in the most cost-effective way.

- **International Emissions Trading (IET)**. Trading of assigned amount units (AAUs) among Annex B countries.
- **Joint Implementation (JI)**. Jointly agreed project investments by one Annex 1 country in another, leading to emission reductions. Emissions savings are measured in emission reduction units (ERUs) which are then credited to and debited against the investing and host country's Kyoto target, respectively.
- **Clean Development Mechanism (CDM)**. Jointly agreed project

investments by Annex 1 countries in non–Annex 1 (developing) countries. Resulting emissions savings are classified as certified emission reductions (CERs) which the investing country can offset against its Kyoto commitments.

Both JI and CDM projects can also be used to create emission removal units (RMUs) for sink enhancement activities. A precursor to JI and CDM was the establishment of 'Activities Implemented Jointly' (AIJ) by the first Conference of Parties (COP-1) to the UNFCCC. Intended as a test phase for joint projects, AIJ does not entail any crediting or transfer of emission credits but provides a valuable insight into opportunities and pitfalls that may be associated with JI in Russia (see Chapter 8).

In theory, AAUs, CERs, ERUs and RMUs are 'fungible' – that is to say, exchangeable. In practice, however, the extent to which individual mechanisms are used will depend on government decisions over their acceptability and use. For example, while the Canadian government may allow companies to trade in AAUs, the EU does not. The following sections elaborate on what these mechanisms may mean for Russia.

International trading of AAUs

International Emissions Trading (IET) under the Kyoto Protocol allows Annex 1 Parties to directly exchange part of their assigned amounts, either by buying surplus allowances from elsewhere to help them meet their targets or by selling any surplus units.

The introduction of emissions trading was one of the most controversial areas of the Kyoto negotiations. Even at the time Kyoto was negotiated, it was apparent that Russia and most other EITs were unlikely to use their full assigned amounts. These unused assigned amounts are somewhat derogatorily termed 'hot air' by Western commentators, reflecting the fact that purchases would yield no environmental benefit as countries were likely to meet their targets anyway. From a Russian perspective, this is unreasonable as the surpluses are a product of painful economic decline and restructuring and thus any benefit from sales should not be considered a 'windfall' but compensation. The West's position is also somewhat hypocritical as other countries such as the UK and Germany also experienced significant emission reductions for reasons unconnected with Kyoto, yet few question that these should be allowed to count against their targets.

Even so, potential buyers of Russia's emission surplus are likely to remain reluctant to buy unused assigned amounts without any tangible environmental benefit. To counter this problem, some have suggested the introduction of a Green Investment Scheme (GIS) – see below.

Joint Implementation

Article 6 of the Kyoto Protocol enables Annex 1 Parties to agree to jointly undertake emissions saving or sink enhancement activities, with credits arising from cross-border investments between Annex 1 Parties to be transferred between them. Annex B Parties may agree jointly to undertake projects that either reduce emissions or increase the removal of greenhouse gases using sinks. It is expected that most of these would take place in EIT countries such as Russia. ERUs generated through JI projects are deducted from the aggregate amount of the host country and added to the aggregate amount of the investing country.

To be eligible under the Kyoto Protocol, a JI project must have the approval of all the parties involved, including the governments of both countries, lead to emission reductions that would not have occurred without the project, and meet other detailed rules as set out in the Marrakech Accords in 2001. Under the Kyoto Protocol, two tracks are defined for JI:

- **Track 1 projects.** In this case, the host country government decides on which projects qualify for ERUs. To qualify for track 1, the host country must meet all eligibility requirements.
- **Track 2 projects.** This requires projects to be evaluated by an independent organization (on top of national approval). Track 2 projects may be possible when Track 1 eligibility criteria are not met.

Which countries are eligible for Track 1 or Track 2 projects will be decided by international negotiators based on the quality of a country's greenhouse gas inventory and reporting systems and may not be known until 2008. It currently seems unlikely that Russia will qualify for Track 1 projects in the near term, but Track 2 projects may be possible (see Chapter 9 for further description of eligibility requirements and eligibility status of Russia).

Russia's interest in JI stems primarily from its need to attract invest-

ment into improving the energy efficiency. For this reason, the concept has attracted the support of both big business and the regions. Official Russian interest in JI has been reconfirmed at recent COPs in statements by Russian delegations. For investors, JI with Russia presents an opportunity to gain significant emission reductions per unit of invest-ment and, perhaps, with a higher return than in the West because of the current low levels of efficiency of some Russian plants. Moreover, JI potentially provides opportunities for domestic businesses and beneficial trade relationships for investors and hosts alike. Host and investor interests in JI are discussed further in Chapter 7.

JI, arguably, offers significantly greater opportunities for Russia than sales of AAUs: benefits accruing to Russia's economy from the sales of AAUs will be determined by the revenue from these sales, while JI projects could involve foreign direct investments significantly larger than the value of the ERUs created by the projects. While the value of ERUs generated by a project will generally not cover the investment costs of a project, it does provide an added incentive to invest in certain types of project, and in a competitive market this could be a decisive factor in investment decisions. Moreover, unlike sales of AAUs, transfers of ERUs would not generally increase the risk of non-compliance with Russia's Kyoto target. However, JI activity in Russia will only be possible if the appro-priate systems for compliance are put in place (see Chapters 9 and 10).

Clean Development Mechanism

The Clean Development Mechanism enables emissions savings or sink enhancement activities to generate certified emission reductions (CERs). Its stated purpose is to help developing countries to achieve sustainable development and to assist Annex 1 countries in achieving compliance. The intention is for a share of the revenues from the CDM to be used to cover administration of the scheme as well as to assist particularly vulnerable developing countries in adapting to climate change.

As Russia is an Annex 1 country, the CDM does not apply to projects it is hosting. Russia could theoretically invest in projects in developing countries, but this seems unlikely since it apparently needs to do nothing to achieve its basic Kyoto commitment (see Chapter 3). Thus the key relevance of the CDM to Russia is the extent to which CDM investments by other Annex 1 countries may affect the market for IET and JI. This is discussed further in Chapter 5.

Limitations

A particular problem for Russia in participating in the project mechanisms is the additionality criterion. Basically this only allows credit for emissions reductions achieved through project activities if the reductions are additional to those which might have occurred otherwise. Additionality is a vague concept and difficult to apply in the case of a transition economy such as Russia's which is undergoing a period of rapid growth and change. Many projects are superficially attractive according to Western economic logic and the lack of capital availability has not been accepted as proof of additionality. However, this ignores the fact that in Russia many other constraints such as institutional and financial problems may prevent the implementation of projects in practice and thus it could be argued that the general Western market logic does not always apply.[1] Indeed, some commentators have suggested capital restriction should be a proof of additionality of a Russian project.[2] Full Track 1 compliance could solve most of Russia's additionality problems as no external verification of a project is required under full compliance, and consequently both investor and host have more flexibility in interpreting what constitutes additionality. This may change if the COP/MOP or the JI Supervisory Committee established at COP/MOP-1 decides on stricter additionality criteria. Such decisions could rule out some Russian projects under Track 2.

Finally, Russian opportunities are likely to be contingent in part on improvements in the business environment. This is notoriously difficult and investors may shy away from the country unless the situation improves or they can obtain risk coverage from institutions such as the EBRD.[3]

Related proposals

Greening AAUs: Green Investment Scheme

The concept of a Green Investment Scheme was formally introduced by Russia at COP-6 in December 2000. Under a GIS, revenues from trading surplus allowances would be earmarked for environmentally related purposes.[4] Thus a GIS could finance a range of activities from capacity building in statistical and reporting methods to large-scale emission reduction projects. Outcomes may or may not be quantifiable,

but the intention is to fund projects which in some way contribute to emission reductions.

Under a GIS, revenues from AAU sales could be put into a carbon fund and then managed/allocated by the Russian government or its appointee. An alternative, proposed by some Russian officials, would be to set up a domestic tender system for allocations. In either case, smaller simple projects could be bundled together as a programme, while large complex projects could be dealt with individually. To set up a well-functioning GIS would require the establishment of an internal organization to host the scheme, and the removal of the many barriers that hold back investments in Russia's energy sector. In addition, other key issues, such as ownership rights to AAUs, also need to be decided. Many of these problems have to be resolved by Russians themselves, and would require support from the highest levels of government, but foreign assistance could also play a role.

In Russia, the idea of a GIS was originally motivated by an ambition to use the revenues from the sale of AAUs to finance investments in energy efficiency. However, other attractions include the possibility of bypassing formal JI channels and greater control over where the resources are allocated. For investors, the attraction would be the opportunity to 'purchase' AAUs in a more politically acceptable way and with a minimum of transaction costs. For those sceptical that Russia will have an emissions surplus, the prospect of selling AAUs with its implicit lowering of the country's target is a concern. This said, a well-run GIS could generate more emission reductions than the AAUs sold, and do so with benefit to the economy.

Discussion of a GIS fell into abeyance during the prolonged uncertainty leading up to Russian ratification of the Kyoto Protocol and no practical steps in developing such a scheme have been taken. However, with the treaty now in force and given the practical and political problems entailed in implementation of unrestricted emissions trading and JI, the idea could be revitalized.

Early Joint Implementation

Given the ongoing major economic reforms in Russia, there would be considerable advantage in enabling JI to be part of this process. However, on the face of it, the Marrakech Accords seem to preclude 'early' JI – that is, the crediting of project-based emission reductions prior to 2008,

although there is some room for debate.[5] In contrast, early (CDM) crediting in developing countries is permitted. This apparent inequity has been one of the contentious aspects of the Protocol for Russia[6] and, on a more practical level, reduces the incentive for early JI investment in Russia. Such issues may be partly resolved through relaxation of the additionality criterion, although this would require international agreement. Already a list of barriers (such as institutional capacity or financial resources) can be used as proof of additionality in the case of small-scale CDM projects.[7]

To address the timing issue, one idea is for host countries such as Russia to use – and for buyers to accept – AAUs as collateral against early emission reductions. Such an approach was endorsed by the World Bank's Prototype Carbon Fund (PCF) as early as June 2000.[8] In this approach, emission reductions generated prior to 2008 in a JI project can be 'guaranteed' by allocations of equivalent quantities of AAUs by the project host country. As emission reductions are verified, they could then be transferred between the registries of the host and the acquiring party as AAUs rather than ERUs. This has the effect of reducing the host's assigned amount for the commitment period while also reducing actual emissions in that country in an independently verified way.

According to the PCF, the Marrakech Accords appear to confirm that this is a legitimate and prudent approach.[9] In other words, if pre-2008 project-based reductions are declared certifiable as ERUs, then Russia and other EITs could attract JI-type investments simply by backing them with AAUs. Though similar to a GIS, in that AAUs provide the means to deliver real emission reductions, early JI is not by definition part of the concept of a GIS.[10] A key difference is that the investment under a GIS derives simply from income from the sale of surplus AAUs, while the FDI involved in JI projects may be far larger than the value of the emissions credits. Nonetheless, many of the points made about GIS crediting apply equally to the PCF scheme. In particular, there is the likely need for some kind of bilateral agreement between Russia and potential foreign partners to set the legal framework for early JI transactions.

Emerging markets

A number of international and domestic markets in carbon emissions are already emerging, both in Kyoto and non-Kyoto countries. How much

Russia will benefit from these developments will depend on how far these schemes allow trading through the international mechanisms and/or link with mutual recognition of each other's schemes. The prospects for the various emerging markets are discussed below.

The EU Emissions Trading Scheme

The EU Emissions Trading Scheme (ETS) is both a vital plank in the EU climate change strategy and the first transnational emissions trading scheme. While the EU ETS is primarily an internal scheme aimed at lowering the costs of compliance for member states, it allows linkage with the other flexible mechanisms via the Linkage Directive. These linkage mechanisms could provide significant benefits for Russia. The EU Greenhouse Gas Emission Allowance Trading Directive[11] establishes a 'cap-and-trade' framework for trading in greenhouse gas emissions across the EU. Under the scheme, total emissions from power- and energy-intensive industries are capped by EU member states and each installation is allocated allowances (EUAs) through a process of National Allocation Plans (NAPs) by which operators can then trade allowances to ensure compliance with their allocations.

The initial phase of the scheme, from 2005 to 2007, covers carbon dioxide emissions from the power sector (all fossil fuel generators over 20MW) and major industrial sectors (oil refining, cement production, iron and steel manufacture, glass and ceramics, and paper and pulp production). Together, these sectors account for 46% of European carbon dioxide emissions. Some 10,000 installations in the 25 EU member states are affected. A second phase will run throughout the Kyoto commitment period from 2008 to 2012, during which time the scheme may be extended to other industry sectors and greenhouse gases (subject to agreement by the European Commission). Further phases of five-year trading periods should continue thereafter, although this will probably depend on international agreement on further emissions constraints.

The EU ETS is linked with the other flexible mechanisms under the Kyoto Protocol via the Linking Directive.[12] Under this Directive, links are initially confined to JI and the CDM. Credits gained from project activities are recognized as equivalent to EUAs and thus can be used by operators to fulfil their obligations under the EU ETS. The possibility of linking with other domestic and international trading schemes via negotiated mutual recognition agreements has been left open. Thus if Russia

established a cap-and-trade system (see below), this could in principle be linked to the EU ETS.

The Linking Directive is intended to encourage JI and CDM investments by EU-based companies in developing countries (through the CDM) and countries such as Russia, Ukraine, Romania and Bulgaria (through JI). Credits from CDM projects can be used from 2005 under prompt start arrangements, but those from JI projects will only be valid from 2008. Member states and operators are required to refrain from the use of credits from nuclear energy. The European Commission will report on necessary requirements with regard to the use of credits generated from sinks in the CDM in 2006. From 2008 member states, in their National Allocation Plans, will have to set a limit on operators' use of the project mechanisms, to ensure that the government's supplementarity obligations are respected.

Ultimately, however, the EU ETS covers only part of the EU-15's commitment to reduce greenhouse gas emissions. Allocations under the NAPs are required to be in line with national commitments, but cover only the traded sectors; member states will need to achieve further emissions reductions domestically or – as a number are doing – seek to use the Kyoto mechanisms to meet their commitments. This provides a significant additional opportunity for Russia.

Carbon funds and tender programmes

Until the launch of the EU ETS, the largest carbon market was in project credits under various carbon funds established by the World Bank and by other multilateral institutions and private entities.[13] Carbon funds are essentially investment channels in which investors are repaid in carbon credits or can use income from credit sales to enhance investment returns. Such funds may simply buy credits or invest directly in projects and claim any emission reductions. For investors these funds can provide a valuable source of emissions credits, with guarantees of Kyoto compliance, while for prospective hosts such as Russia they can not only provide a market for projects but frequently give support and guidance in project development.

The World Bank offers a suite of carbon funds, the most long-established of which is the Prototype Carbon Fund, launched in 2000. With the entry into force of the Kyoto Protocol and the launch of the EU ETS, the number of funds available has burgeoned as both

governments and business turn to carbon funds to source emissions credits. A number of countries, including the Netherlands, Austria and Belgium, also operate government tender programmes and facilities under which prospective JI or CDM hosts are invited to submit proposals for emission reduction projects. These programmes, together with the carbon funds, offer significant opportunities for Russia to attract investment into energy efficiency and other emissions reduction projects, and are discussed further in Chapter 7.

Other potential markets

A number of countries apart from EU member states are in the process of developing, or considering, domestic emissions trading schemes which may, over time, provide further opportunities for Russia.[14] Launched in 2002, the UK's voluntary emissions trading scheme is the world's most long-established greenhouse gas programme. It overlaps with the EU ETS in terms of both time and participants. Norway too is considering developing its own ETS and then potentially linking this to the EU ETS. The EU has declared that its ETS directive is relevant to the European Economic Area (EEA) and normally this would mean that Norway (as an EEA member) would adopt it and transpose the provisions into national legislation. However, Norway is reluctant to do this because of differences in emissions profiles and the revenues it receives from carbon taxation.[15] The Canadians are proposing a nationwide emissions trading scheme in which initiators of environmentally friendly projects could earn credits for sale to big industrial emitters or the federal government.[16]

Further opportunities for Russia may arise even from non-Kyoto countries. In Australia, the New South Wales greenhouse gas abatement scheme started in January 2003 and is now in force until 2012. Under this scheme, utilities are set benchmarks which they are then required to meet by offsetting their emissions through tradable credits. Within the United States, individual states are also seeking to reduce their emissions through trading. More than half of the US states have adopted green-house gas regulations or are in the process of dong so.[17] New Hampshire, Massachusetts, Maine, California, New Jersey and New York are among those that have established state-wide or sectoral targets, while Oregon and Washington (state) require utilities to offset a portion of greenhouse gas emissions from new facilities. Nine states in the northeast and midwest are also cooperating in a 'Regional Greenhouse Gas Initiative'

to control carbon dioxide from power plants. The Chicago Climate Exchange (CCX) is a pilot greenhouse gas cap-and-trade scheme. Under the CCX, entities – mainly US firms – have agreed to voluntarily limit greenhouse gas emissions from 2003 to 2006.[18]

Prospects for US-wide emissions trading remain some way off. Proposals for a national cap-and-trade emissions trading scheme have twice been rejected by the US Senate.[19] However, in June 2005 the Senate adopted a resolution affirming the science of climate change and calling, for the first time, for mandatory market-based limits on emissions and incentives for emissions reductions. Though non-binding, this suggests some impetus to reduce emissions and a continued interest in market-based mechanisms. For now, however, the greatest opportunities in the US are likely to arise from developments at state level.

Finally, there is an emerging 'retail market' for emissions credits for individuals and companies that wish to be 'climate neutral' (that is, to offset their emissions through either emission reduction projects or sinks projects) for reasons of social responsibility or public relations. Though generally not intended for compliance, this is a small but growing market and may support significant emission reduction projects.

Such domestic, state and private schemes could potentially provide a market for Russia's emissions allowances and credits in future if appropriately linked or accredited. However, while this may be fairly straightforward on a technical level, it would be politically difficult, particularly with respect to non-Kyoto parties. A key issue would be maintaining the environmental integrity of such an arrangement when some parties do not have established caps. Furthermore, the notion of transactions between individual states and countries is also likely to raise questions over sovereignty.

A Russian emissions trading scheme?

A further way for Russia to benefit from emissions trading would be to set up its own domestic cap-and-trade scheme and link this to other international schemes. Ideally, Russia's allowances captured under a domestic ETS would be fully fungible with EU allowances. The advantage of such a scheme over JI is that additionality would be less of an issue and an ETS would avoid the high transaction costs associated with JI. In theory at least, a Russian ETS could also coexist alongside a GIS.

To create a domestic ETS, the Russian government would need to set a cap on carbon dioxide emissions of domestic companies, allocate allowances to companies and then authorize them to trade these allowances internationally. This process could easily take a couple of years. It would require not just changes in Russian laws and regulations requiring mandatory monitoring and reporting of greenhouse gas emissions, but also the establishment of a legal framework, agreement over sectors to be covered and distribution of institutional responsibilities and creation of principles for distribution of emission rights and their transfer.[20]

Experience from the EU ETS and other OECD countries highlights the complexity and sensitivity of debates around national allocation plans. An industry-wide scheme may be resisted on grounds that it could be a precursor to tighter caps from 2012. Indeed, Czech companies opposed the idea even though they stood to gain more than they would lose from implementation of the EU ETS. A more workable option in the first instance may be to set up a smaller scheme around just one or two companies, for example Gazprom and/or Russia's electricity monopoly, RAO UES.[21]

Any domestic Russian ETS is likely to require both internal and international political support. Although scheme design and allocations would primarily be issues for the Russian government, any plan would also have to be seen as credible to potential buyers if allowances were to be traded internationally. More generally, Russia would also need to agree rules and procedures for linking its domestic ETS with the EU ETS or any other trading schemes. In any case, fungibility with the EU ETS may only be possible from 2008.

Taken together, these points suggest that some form of limited industry-specific emissions trading scheme could emerge in Russia in time for the first Kyoto commitment period.

State of the market

A World Bank study in May 2005 on trends in the carbon market shows that the carbon market is expanding steadily: $107mtCO_2e$ were exchanged through projects in 2004[22] – a 38% increase on 2003. While historically the bulk of trade has been through project transactions, allowance-based transactions formed the fastest-growing part of the

market. The volume of assets exchanged through the allowance markets in early 2005 was comparable with that arising from project transactions. This development was driven largely by the start of the EU ETS in January 2005.

While this growth in the market should provide opportunities for Russia, it has yet to register significantly in the emerging markets. In 2004 and early 2005, the principal project suppliers were concentrated in a few countries, notably India, China and Brazil; less than 10% of project volumes were in the transition economies. The lack of trade with Russia is not surprising given the uncertainty over whether or not it would ratify the Kyoto Protocol during this time. However, continuing slowness over implementation threatens to undermine investor confidence. It is notable that whereas Russia signed its first deal with Denmark in summer 2005, by September UES was expressing concern that if the government failed to approve the project by late October, the whole deal could founder.[23]

There are now a multitude of buyers in the Kyoto markets. Between 2004 and early 2005, private and public entities in Europe made up 60% of the volume of emission reductions in the project markets. The EU ETS is the largest of the four active allowance markets. More than half of the projects were related to non-CO_2 reductions, with the greatest volumes of emissions reductions being associated with projects aimed at destroying HFC_{23}, a very powerful greenhouse gas. Traditional energy-efficiency and fuel-switching projects made up just 5% of the market. Prices for project-based emissions reductions achieved were in the order of US$4–5. This is significantly lower than for early trades under the EU ETS, where prices are not simply higher but increased from around €7–9 in 2004 to €17 in spring 2005. This price differential largely reflects the higher level of risk associated with projects as compared with allowance trading.

On the surface, the relatively low level of apparent interest in energy projects and low carbon prices is disturbing news for Russia given its huge interest in energy projects. However, the current market is inevitably a reflection of where investors feel they can gain the greatest credits with least effort; it does not reflect the scope for future investments in the energy sector. Indeed as the markets grow, investors will necessarily be compelled to look around more widely and prices are expected to rise.

Longer-term opportunities

Although the focus of this book is on Russian opportunities during the first Kyoto commitment period from 2008 to 2012, the current set of targets was intended to represent just a first step in a dynamic evolving regime. Under the Kyoto Protocol, Parties were required to start negotiations on future (post-2012) commitments by 2005. While further commitments are likely to require much more stringent emission reductions, considerable uncertainty persists over the shape and form they may take and the role of the Kyoto mechanisms. This uncertainty not only affects longer-term carbon markets but casts a shadow over existing efforts to reduce emissions and could undermine the incentive for Parties to deliver on existing commitments.

International negotiations will be long and arduous, not least because of the political and environmental necessity of engaging the US and, over time, the more advanced developing countries (such as China, India, Brazil, South Korea, Mexico and South Africa). While it is commonly assumed that future commitments will take the form of binding caps, other models – or steps – are possible. In particular, if emissions trading succeeds in delivering low-cost reductions in emissions, then it is possible to envisage progressive globalization of emissions trading through regional and bilateral agreements and/or internal schemes by multinational companies.

While the EU ETS is currently expected to continue with a ratcheting down of emissions limits, other Kyoto mechanisms are likely to be re-evaluated in the light of experience. Already, significant scepticism exists over the long-term viability of the project mechanisms in their current form, owing to difficulties in proving additionality, and high transaction costs. One idea currently gaining currency is the possibility of sectoral-level – as opposed to project-level – CDM (an idea which could also apply to JI).

What this means for Russia is unclear. While there is no reason to believe that Russia should not succeed in achieving favourable treatment in negotiations over future commitments, the pressure will be on to deliver tangible reductions in emissions, particularly since this appears to be in Russia's wider economic interest. The challenge for Russia and the international community is thus to capitalize upon the existing mechanisms to deliver both reductions in emissions and the investment in the energy sector that the country sorely needs.

Conclusions

The emerging markets in carbon offer significant, and growing, opportunities to reduce emissions of greenhouse gases in a cost-effective way, with major potential markets for credits emerging through the EU ETS and other allowance-based schemes and through carbon funds and tender schemes. While project investments represent the most immediate prospects for Russia, further opportunities could arise through the development of a domestic trading scheme which could later be linked to other national schemes, and/or through furthering ideas of a GIS. However, capitalizing upon these benefits will require Russian compliance with the Kyoto Protocol and its effective administration. The potential value of these opportunities to Russia is discussed in the following chapters, together with the prospects for compliance.

5 THE VALUE TO RUSSIA OF EMISSIONS TRADING

Under the Kyoto mechanisms, Russia will be entitled to sell any surplus of its assigned amount over actual emissions. Chapter 3 showed that under most economic growth scenarios, Russia's 2008–12 greenhouse gas emissions will be lower than 1990 levels. This means that Russia will almost certainly have emissions quotas available to sell.

The value of Russia's surplus will depend on numerous factors, including the size of surplus; the design of the trading mechanisms; potential demand levels, degree of competition from other countries and strategic behaviour of both buyers and sellers; and the extent to which the project mechanisms are used. This chapter assesses these factors and provides a review of literature on potential carbon prices, together with results from an analysis of the likely value of Russia's surplus under various growth, trade and market scenarios.

Russia's surplus

The potential size of Russia's surplus under the 14 economic growth/ energy intensity scenarios presented in CEPA (2004) (see Chapter 3) are set out in Table 5.1. These scenarios suggest that Russia could have an emissions surplus of up to 400 million tonnes of carbon equivalent (MtCe) over the first commitment period under the Kyoto Protocol, with most scenarios suggesting a potential surplus of 150–300 MtCe. The only circumstances under which Russia might need to be a net buyer of others' surpluses would be if Putin's growth challenge were achieved despite low levels of improvements in energy efficiency, or if 4% growth were achieved with no reduction in energy intensity. As discussed in Chapter 3, both scenarios are considered highly unlikely.

Table 5.2 compares CEPA's estimate of Russia's surplus with those from Russian and other international sources. They show a wide variation,

Table 5.1: Russia's surplus of greenhouse gas emissions (MtCe), 2008–12

(a) Assuming significant implementation of reforms

Energy intensity reduction (%)	Economic growth (%)			
	7.2	6	4	2
High: 4	207–131	248–206	314–311	406–368
Low: 2	95–(-65)	143–30	218–169	286–285

(b) Assuming little or no implementation of reforms

Energy intensity reduction (%)	Economic growth (%)		
	4	2	0
High: 2	218–169	286–285	384–347
Low: 0	110–(-13)	189–136	261–261

Source: CEPA (2004).

with the highest estimate, from Point Carbon, being a surplus of over 1,300 MtCe. In general, Russian estimates tend to be lower than international ones, probably reflecting more optimistic growth expectations and/or lower improvements in energy intensity. CEPA's estimates tend towards the low end of the remaining assessments and thus could be considered very conservative.

Trading mechanisms

The value of Russia's emissions surplus derives from use of the flexible mechanisms set up under the Kyoto Protocol and will depend on the structure of the mechanisms used and the way they are implemented. As discussed in Chapter 4, Annex 1 Parties may trade assigned amount units (AAUs) either *directly* through international emissions trading (IET), where countries directly exchange AAUs, or *indirectly*, through Joint Implementation, where a country invests in a project in another country and gains a reduction in AAUs as a result. Direct emissions trading is undertaken by countries with governments striking deals over AAU

Table 5.2: Estimates of Russia's surplus greenhouse gas emissions (MtCe)

Origin	Year	Surplus
Russian		
2nd National Communication to UNFCCC	2002	340
Ministry of Economic Development and Trade	2003	408–545
3rd National Communication to UNFCCC	2003	456–913
International		
International Energy Agency	2004	817
Point Carbon	2003	1362
CEPA		
Full range	2004	(-65)–406
Mid-range	2004	150–300

Sources: Adapted from CMS and DKW Equity Research in Mielke et al. (2004), and CEPA (2004).

transactions. However, countries can also draw up frameworks which allow companies to carry out trade of AAUs. In theory, the end result of allowing governments and companies to trade should be the same; in practice, they may not be.

The structure of the mechanisms, and the way in which governments choose to implement them, mean that in reality there is no single value to emission units; it depends on who is selling, and in what form. Emission units are 'tagged' in the registration process, and government rules mean that exchanges of different types of units may not be possible. However, it seems likely that pressures on Annex 1 Parties to meet their Kyoto targets may lead to the establishment of greater linkages between these different markets.

Thus the value of Russia's surplus will not be determined by a perfectly competitive market, but by markets subject to rules that have yet to be created. Key determinants will be:

- whether governments will directly purchase AAUs;
- whether established trading mechanisms will allow the purchase

of emissions surpluses, directly or indirectly, through the method of linking with other markets;

• the volume made available.

The impact of government decisions will be discussed below.

Potential buyers

At present, the United States and Australia are very unlikely to ratify the Protocol, although Australia has indicated that it will in any event seek to meet its Kyoto commitments. This means that the main potential buyers of Russia's emissions surplus are the EU member states, other European countries (e.g. Norway and Switzerland), Japan and Canada.

While direct trading of AAUs is an attractive option for Russia as it would be the simplest way to monetize its surplus, most countries remain wary of simply purchasing surplus AAUs without conditions attached. The implied simple transfers of wealth without any direct environmental benefit could prove to be politically unacceptable, thus limiting the market for Russia's surplus.

In any case, the scope for countries to use emissions trading to meet their targets – and thus the market for Russia's surplus – may be restricted by the 'supplementarity' principle within the Kyoto Protocol. This requires use of the Kyoto mechanisms to be supplementary to domestic action. The supplementary requirement is a loosely defined concept but is commonly interpreted as limiting the use of the Kyoto mechanisms to 50% of any shortfall in AAUs under 'business-as-usual' scenarios (that is, if no action had been taken to reduce emissions).

European Union

The EU's collective target under the Kyoto Protocol of an 8% net reduction in greenhouse gas emissions on 1990 levels applies to the 15 states which were members of the EU prior to May 2004 (the EU-15). Individual country targets have been assigned through a burden-sharing agreement. Eight of the ten states that joined the EU in May 2004 are subject to individual Kyoto targets, while Cyprus and Malta have no targets.

The original EU-15 and new member states have different interests in application of the Kyoto mechanisms. The EU-15 are potential purchasers

of credit, while most of the new accession states are potential suppliers of credits. In 2002, the EU-15 was little more than a third of the way towards reaching its collective target, and only three of its members are on course to meet their target through domestic implementation alone.[1] In contrast, all of the new member states – with the exception of Slovenia – were on track to meet or exceed their commitments.

The EU-15's efforts to meet their Kyoto commitments are focused on domestic implementation. A key plank in their strategy is the development of an internal market for emissions trading – the EU ETS. Under this scheme, AAUs cannot be sold directly to companies as AAUs cannot be converted into EU allowances (EUAs) and are not valid for compliance. Thus, any benefit to Russia from the EU ETS will be associated with indirect trades through JI projects under the Linking Directive.

This said, the EU ETS applies only to the traded sector and member states remain free to trade AAUs through bilateral agreements. In general, both the EU and its member states are resistant to the idea of the use of 'ungreened' AAUs. Policies adopted by individual states, such as the Dutch CERUPT and ERUPT programmes which are designed for acquiring credits through CDM and JI respectively, also suggest a preference for project-based trading. However, there are no legal requirements to prevent EU member states from buying surplus AAUs. In practice, EU use of Kyoto units will be shaped not simply by price but also by wider political and strategic considerations, such as the desire to reduce poverty in Africa and to enhance cooperation between industry and the government.

Japan

Japan has adopted a very ambitious greenhouse gas reduction target, in particular taking into account the high energy efficiency levels already existing in the country. In fact, analysts point out that Japanese business feels somewhat misled by the Kyoto process – targets in Japan are generally used to signal direction as opposed to being mandatory obligations.[2]

While Japan's focus is on domestic implementation, it is actively seeking ways of meeting its commitments through the Kyoto mechanisms and in doing so is likely to exercise buyer sovereignty over where, with whom and in what it invests.[3] Currently, Japanese implementation plans do not formally include any use of Russia's allowances. The prolonged economic stagnation in Japan makes it difficult to persuade

the sceptics concerned about Japan's economic wellbeing that resource transfers to Russia, for example, would be in Japanese interests. In any case, NGO pressure will lead Japan to seek to ensure that trading is tied to environmental achievement and this will constrain its ability to purchase surplus allowances.

Japan demonstrated its interest in projects with Russia over JI as far back as 1998 when the government announced 20 'AIJ' projects. However, the failure of these projects to materialize has left Japan frustrated and sceptical over Russia's reliability as a source of credits. Even so, Japanese companies are actively exploring JI options with Russia. This trend is strengthened by Japan's desire to forge better energy links between the two countries owing to its dependency on energy imports and instability in the Middle East. Nevertheless Japan also recognizes the value of the CDM as an instrument for gaining credits and is active in developing this option.

Canada

Canada probably faces even greater problems in meeting its Kyoto commitments domestically than Japan (in percentage terms) and is ideologically inclined towards emissions trading. Even so, the Canadians are subject to the same political concerns as other countries about buying 'ungreened' AAUs from Russia. Both environmental NGOs and the public strongly object to the idea of giving Russia money for what they see as 'doing nothing'. Canadian companies have more mixed interests in Kyoto: while many would prefer not to have to constrain emissions, some see the project mechanisms as a means to benefit Canadian industry. A similar range of climatic conditions means that Canadian expertise could be very valuable to Russia as it seeks to modernize its ageing infrastructure and some have mooted the possibility of linking trading schemes between Russia and Alberta.

If the Canadian government does decide to purchase AAUs as a means of meeting its Kyoto targets, it is most likely that any major purchases would be concluded on a negotiated basis between the Canadian and Russian governments. Informed commentators point out that at present political constraints on the Canadian government seem likely to place considerable downward pressures on the level of any negotiated price,[4] although this situation could change towards the end of the first commitment period.

The Canadian government has indicated that it will recognize AAUs

within its planned domestic ETS. However, there is also a real possibility that Canada may link into the EU ETS. Given that Russia's emissions surplus cannot be converted directly into the European carbon currency, the Canadian demand for Russia's emissions surplus would then be suppressed as Canadian companies begin trading on the EU ETS.

Competitors

Russia will face competition in the international carbon markets from other economies in transition (EITs). Under the Kyoto Protocol, most central and east European countries agreed to go along with the EU commitment of an 8% emissions reduction on 1990 levels. Ukraine, like Russia, insisted on a right to return emissions to 1990 levels. As in Russia, emissions from other EITs fell dramatically in the transition from central planning to a market economy and the associated economic contraction. Emissions for all EITs, with the exception of Slovenia, were well below their base levels in 2000, implying a substantial surplus under Kyoto.[5] Like Russia, the EITs are also eligible for JI projects.

Ukraine is potentially the second largest source of surplus emissions after Russia and the relationship between these two countries could be critical in determining the availability of surplus. Demand for Russia's surplus could be further undermined by the EU accession countries, which collectively have an emissions 'headroom' about as large as the shortfall in the original EU-15 member states.

Other potential competitors in the Kyoto markets are developing countries. While they do not have a 'surplus' to sell as they currently have no emissions targets, the CDM can be used to generate emissions credits which Annex 1 countries can offset against their assigned amounts. Competition from these countries and the other EITs will inevitably reduce the demand for, and the value of, Russia's surplus.

Impact of JI and CDM

Direct trading of Russia's surplus will be affected by the extent to which Annex 1 countries choose to use the project mechanisms to achieve their Kyoto commitments. In practice, it is simply another form of transferring credits between countries that normally trade with each other, as JI is only possible among Annex 1 countries. However, the CDM is different

in that it provides an alternative mechanism to offset emissions from Annex 1 countries.

In the past, uncertainty over the fate of the Kyoto Protocol reduced the incentive for companies to participate in the CDM and JI, and their application was limited to the World Bank's carbon funds and government tender programmes (see Chapter 4). However, the treaty's entry into force, combined with agreement over the EU's Linking Directive, is likely to boost demand from companies and governments alike.

Most estimates of potential demand for JI and CDM suggest that the market could be fairly small, with projects amounting to between 200 and 300 MtCO$_2$e (or 54–81 MtCe) in total.[6] In practice, demand could be much greater than this, judging by the distance of key actors from their Kyoto targets and (at least in the case of Japan) the high domestic abatement costs. Indeed in late 2005, EU member states alone planned to purchase almost 520 MtCO$_2$e (or 142 MtCe) for 2008–12 both via multilateral programmes and individually.[7] This is in addition to private-sector investments through the EU ETS. The scope for and value of JI to Russia are examined in depth in Chapter 7.

Strategic behaviour

With the withdrawal of the US from the Kyoto Protocol, the supply of emissions allowances and credits is likely to greatly exceed demand. Russia (along with other countries with surplus emissions, such as Ukraine) may therefore try to control the supply of AAUs into the market, with a view to increasing the unit prices. A review of many of the studies on the strategic nature of emissions trading is contained in Bernard et al. (2003). These studies indicate that:

- Russia has an incentive to delay the sale of emissions surplus. A late upsurge in demand as the commitment period approaches – and/or the US rejoining the system – would mean Russia may be the only major source of AAUs.
- In contrast, consideration of fossil fuel markets may give Russia an incentive to release more credits, because credit availability would reduce the need for cuts in emissions elsewhere and thus help maintain fossil fuel demand. (The impact of emissions trading on fossil fuel exports is considered in Chapter 6.)

- With the United States out of the Kyoto Protocol, it is optimal for Russia and Ukraine to sell only about 50% of their surplus emissions quota. Restricting supply helps keep prices high while not curtailing fossil fuel demand too much.
- Restricting the sale of AAUs could increase demand for JI projects and thus support Russian engagement in the EU ETS.[8]

A further, related, consideration for Russia is the option to 'bank' some or all of its emissions surplus as part of a deliberate strategy to restrict supply or to hold against future emission obligations, or simply as a result of non-use. Under the Kyoto Protocol, emission surpluses not used in the first commitment period can be carried forward to future commitment periods. Such unused surpluses would have a value, although this is difficult to quantify. For one thing, it is not yet clear whether there will be a second commitment period. For another, the value of surpluses will depend on numerous unknown factors, including the level of commitments by Russia and other countries to reduce emissions further. Moreover, if a surplus were also expected in the second commitment period, the value of these credits would not be realized until the third period.

The risks associated with banked emissions suggest that while they may indeed have a value, it should have a high discount rate. In any case, the extent to which surplus emissions units can be sold will be determined not only by Russia's strategic behaviour but also by the willingness of others to buy.

International carbon prices

Levels of participation in the Kyoto markets and strategic behaviour will critically influence the price of carbon and thus the value of Russia's surplus. Many studies of the potential development of emissions trading under the Kyoto mechanisms have been published. They give a wide range of estimates of carbon prices, reflecting both the nature of the model used[9] and other assumptions made. A summary and review of 25 of these models is set out in Springer (2003). Assuming that the US participates in the Kyoto markets, these studies suggest that:

- **If all countries trade**, then permit prices could be in the range of US\$1–22/tonne CO_2 (US\$4–80/tC), with an average price of

US$9/tCO$_2$ (US$33/tC). Total permits traded would be in the range of 1,214–3,428 MtCO$_2$ (331–935 MtC).

- **If trade is restricted to Annex 1 countries** – that is with no CDM – then the permit price could be much higher, with an average price of US$27/tCO$_2$ (US$99/tC). Again the range of prices is very large – US$3–71/tCO$_2$ (US$11–260/tC).

Given the US withdrawal from the Kyoto Protocol, such prices are unrealistically high. Studies which exclude the US as a potential purchaser point to substantially lower permit prices – in the range of US$0–12/tCO$_2$ (US$0–44/tC). In combination with the limits on credits from sinks, the conclusion drawn by Springer is that the 'permit prices approach zero'. However, oligopolistic behaviour by the major sellers of permits – Russia, Ukraine, and east European countries – could increase permit prices, with studies suggesting a range of US$7–12/tCO$_2$ (US$26–44/tC).

Modelled value of Russia's surplus

As discussed above, the value of emissions trading to Russia will depend on a range of factors. CEPA (2004) have undertaken a detailed analysis of the potential value of emissions trading to Russia under a range of economic growth, emissions surplus trade and market structure scenarios.[10] To do this, they use a specially tailored version of the Carbon Emission Reduction Trading (CERT) model. This model uses an assessment of the projections of emissions by groups of countries under a business-as-usual scenario, distance from their Kyoto targets, and the estimated costs of reducing emissions to calculate the likely equilibrium price of emission units. The model is used to test different assumptions about strategic behaviour.

CERT, in common with many other models, makes a number of implicit assumptions about the way in which the market will work, as well as the underlying technical parameters and costs driving the market. In particular, in the model there is no distinction between trading of emissions credits undertaken by companies through emissions markets, by countries at the level of AAUs, or in the CDM and JI markets. In the real world, these distinctions are important and, as noted above, there can be different prices in the different markets. However, the model does

provide a useful guide as to the price at which Russia could sell AAUs, and the factors determining that price.

Scenarios

CEPA use three different types of scenarios to examine the benefits to Russia of emissions trading.

- **Growth scenarios**. These assess the impact of alternative scenarios of Russia's economic growth and energy/carbon intensity on Russia's carbon emissions (and thus the likely size of its surplus). Of the 14 scenarios discussed in Chapter 3 and used to calculate this surplus (see Table 5.1), CEPA selected four of the most plausible combinations for this analysis. These are shown in Table 5.3, together with projected carbon emissions.

Table 5.3: Growth scenarios

	Reform – moderate	Reform – Putin's challenge	No reform – moderate	No reform – critical
Growth (%)	4	7.2	2	0
Energy intensity (%)	2	4	2	0
Projected emissions (MtC)	638	661	546	570

Source: CEPA (2004).

- **Emissions surplus trade scenarios.** These scenarios demonstrate the impact of various restrictions on supply of emissions credits. In the model, supply constraints are represented by caps on exports of: 0% (closed restricted market); 20% (open restricted market), 60% (open market), 100% (open liberal market). The introduction of caps effectively reduces the supply of credits and thus

pushes up the equilibrium price as demand has to be met (i.e. all the Annex B countries are legally obligated to meet their Kyoto targets).

- **Market structure scenarios.** These examine the impact of varying levels of international participation in emissions trading on equilibrium price and on Russia. Three scenarios were modelled:
  (i) 'all countries trade', including the EU;
  (ii) 'trade without the EU', thus restricting demand to Japan and other OECD countries;
  (iii) 'trade without the EU and EET3' (the non-EU east European transition economies – Bulgaria, Romania and Croatia), thus removing a source of both demand and supply.

All three scenarios assume that the US is not a participant.

The carbon emissions outputs from the four growth scenarios are used as inputs into the CERT model. These are then run concurrently with three emissions surplus trade and four market structure scenarios to generate 48 results. Each of the results comprises two elements – total financial benefit to Russia, and world equilibrium price for emissions credits. All of the model runs assume that other Annex B countries continue to produce emissions at current levels and that only 10% of CDM projects are successfully realized.

Demand and supply

Under all four growth scenarios, Russia is a net supplier (seller) of credits as its emissions in 2010 are projected to be below its Kyoto target. (The situation where Russia is a net buyer of credits is not modelled as this is regarded as highly unlikely.) Moreover, Russia's surplus is available at lower cost than the sum of the other suppliers (Ukraine and the EET3). Figure 5.1 shows net demanders and suppliers of emissions credits in the Kyoto market under the *reform – moderate growth* scenario. In this scenario, Japan is the main potential buyer of emissions. The EU demand level is shown as uncertain owing to the potential influence of JI and the EU ETS.

The supply and demand schedules which give rise to the world equilibrium price of emissions credits and the quantity of carbon abatement traded in the market are illustrated in Figure 5.2. This graph depicts the scenario that results in the greatest net benefit to Russia – the *no reform – moderate growth* scenario, combined with a 20% export cap on

Figure 5.1: Annual abatement requirement

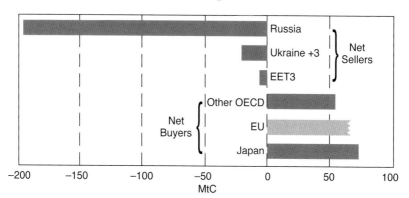

Source: CEPA (2004).

Note: Six individual or groups of countries are distinguished: (i) the EU (the EU-15 plus the eight accession countries with Kyoto targets, i.e. not Malta and Cyprus); (ii) Japan; (iii) Other OECD (Australia, Canada, Iceland, New Zealand, Norway and Switzerland – but excluding the US as a market participant); (iv) Russia; (v) Ukraine plus Lithuania, Latvia and Estonia; (vi) three east European transition economies (EET3) – Croatia, Bulgaria and Romania.

Figure 5.2: Illustrative demand and supply curve

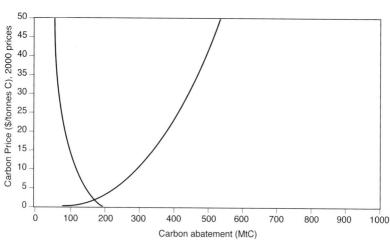

Source: CEPA (2004).

emissions surplus trade, and with all country groups trading. The upward sloping curve is the supply of credits in the market derived from the summated marginal abatement cost curves of the individual groups, and the downward sloping curve is the world demand for carbon reduction at each price. The intersection of the two curves establishes an equilibrium price of US$3.3/tC of abatement.

Model results

Results from the 48 scenarios are summarized in Table 5.4. For each growth scenario, the high and low estimates of carbon price and benefits to Russia across the full range of market and trade scenarios are shown, together with the conditions required to maximize the benefits to Russia.

Table 5.4: Value to Russia of emissions trading under various growth, trade and market structure scenarios

Growth scenario	Benefit to Russia (US$ million)		Equilibrium price (US$/tC)		Assumptions required to maximize benefit	
	Low	High	Low	High	Export cap?	EU trade?
Reform – moderate	0	243	0.0	4.0	Yes, 20%	Yes
Reform – Putin's challenge	0	245	0.0	4.2	Yes, 20%	Yes
No reform – moderate	0	255	0.0	3.3	Yes, 20%	Yes
No reform – critical	0	254	0.0	3.5	Yes, 20%	Yes

Source: CEPA (2004).

A key finding is that in the absence of the US, Russia is unlikely to derive much – if any – benefit from emissions trading. In an unrestricted market, the value of the benefits to Russia under a wide range of scenarios is zero. The maximum benefit is in the order of US$250 million under all four growth scenarios. This is because without the US, there is insufficient net demand for credits to absorb the surplus of Russia and Ukraine and thus to set a higher value on carbon. Market prices for

emissions credits generally range between US$0 and just over US$4/tC across the various scenarios.[11] These are broadly consistent with – albeit at the low end of – findings of other studies of international carbon prices discussed earlier.

A further important finding is that for Russia to benefit, the EU almost certainly has to be actively involved in emissions trading. Without the EU, the demand side of the market collapses unless a tight export cap on emissions surplus trading is implemented and strictly enforced among the Annex B countries. The inclusion of the EU in the global trading system (that is, allowing the EU to purchase emissions surpluses) raises the value of credits and thus the potential benefit to Russia.

The results further highlight just how important the export cap is for Russia to realize a benefit from trading. Restrictions on trade in emissions surpluses drive up the price of carbon to a level that enables Russia to profit from trading. Under all four growth scenarios, Russia gains most when a 20% cap is applied and the supply of credits is highly restricted. Despite this, the potential value of trading to Russia is not large. Putin's *challenge growth* scenario is the only growth scenario under which Russia can benefit from trading without an export cap. This is because there is a critical level of projected emissions in 2010 beyond which an export cap is no longer required – the supply of Russia's emissions surplus is sufficiently restricted by its own increased carbon emissions for no export cap to be necessary to enable Russia to accrue benefit from trading. Even so, this would require EU participation – or US re-entry into the Kyoto system.

As in the case of other model experiments, such findings cannot be taken as a definitive assessment of the likely development of emissions trading, but do provide insights into the determinants of emission values using the (simplistic) assumption of a perfectly competitive emissions market. Still more fundamentally, all this assumes Russia will be prepared to sell its surplus.

Impact of US non-participation

The above analyses assume that the US will not participate in international trading. For comparative purposes, CEPA carried out a brief modelling exercise to ascertain the benefit to Russia if the US were to be part of the trading regime.[12] This serves both to demonstrate the significance for Russia of the US withdrawal and to indicate something of the

potential should the US engage in international trading at some future date.

Two scenarios are considered. In the first, world demand for credits in the absence of the US is assumed to be about 200 MtC in 2010. The second scenario assumes world demand will total about 670 MtC in 2010 because of US participation. In addition, both scenarios assume:

(i) Russia's GDP growth of 4%;

(ii) Russia's energy intensity reduction of 2% (i.e. the *reform – moderate growth* scenario);

(iii) 60% of supply-side countries' emissions surplus is available for trade.

Findings under both scenarios are shown in Table 5.5.

Table 5.5: Annual benefit to Russia in 2010

Scenario	World equilibrium price (US$/tC)	Potential benefit to Russia (US$ million)
US out	1.3	161
US in	25.1	4,390

Source: CEPA (2004).

The devastating impact of US withdrawal on world carbon prices is immediately clear from these findings, as they plummet from US$25 to just over US$1/tC and the potential benefit to Russia decreases from over US$4 billion to just US$160 million. While the US is highly unlikely to ratify the Kyoto Protocol, Russia may recoup a small part of the lost benefit through ongoing developments in state- and company-level trading schemes, or some future federal trading scheme (such as that proposed by Senators McCain and Lieberman – see Chapter 4). Much would, however, depend on the design of the mechanisms.

'Real world' value of emissions trading

While the above modelling analyses indicate that the price for Russia's surplus is likely to be very low, this is not a realistic basis for assessing the value of that surplus. Quite simply, with a price close to zero Russia

would have no incentive to sell. Indeed, it could do better to take a chance on banking its surplus despite uncertainties over its future value.

In the real world, however, it is likely that carbon deals will be done between Annex 1 countries at risk of exceeding their Kyoto targets and countries with surpluses. As indicated earlier, while demand for emissions surplus is currently very weak, it could well intensify towards the end of the first commitment period as countries find themselves unable to meet their Kyoto targets in other ways. It also seems highly unlikely that the 'free market' will determine the price of the AAUs to be traded. Rather, trades will most probably take place through political negotiations and be linked to other economic and geopolitical considerations.

To give an idea of this value, CEPA calculate the benefit to Russia at two potentially negotiated prices – US$7.5/tC and US$20/tC – for a range of global negotiation levels. This is probably reasonably indicative of the price range within which deals might be struck. Though higher than the 'free market' prices indicated above, this range reflects the needs of sellers to achieve a positive price while also remaining attractive to prospective purchasers as they are still well below the likely international carbon price for project credits.

For simplicity, negotiated sales for Russia's surplus are expressed as an aggregate percentage of the global carbon abatement reduction (rather than in terms of bilateral deals) and set at 10–50% of the global abatement requirement. Again, the assumption is that the US would not participate in international emissions trading and that demand from other OECD countries and the EU would be approximately 200 MtC in 2010. Table 5.6 shows the estimated negotiable revenues to Russia under the different price and demand scenarios. With a range of percentages of global carbon abatement set at between 10% and 50%, revenues to Russia range

Table 5.6: Estimated negotiable revenues (US$ billion)

| US$/tonne C | Negotiated % of global carbon abatement requirement | | | | |
	10	20	30	40	50
7.5	0.15	0.30	0.45	0.59	0.74
20	0.40	0.79	1.19	1.58	1.98

Source: CEPA (2004).

elasticities between fuels.[1] There will also be different effects in the short and long term as, for example, investment in electricity generation plants by energy-intensive industries responds to the new price differentials.[2] The following sections examine the effects of the Kyoto Protocol on the oil and gas markets and make an overall assessment of the possible impact on the overall value of Russia's fossil fuel exports.

Oil markets

Barker et al. (2001) contains a survey of numerous analyses of the potential impacts of measures to mitigate climate change. As with the estimates of the value of carbon prices (see Chapter 5), a wide range of

Table 6.1: Impacts on projected international oil demand and revenues

Study	Impact on world projected oil demand	Comment
Pershing (2000)	7–13% decline	In trading scenarios only. Survey of other model results.
McKibben et al. (1999)	7% decline	25% reduction reported with no trading.
Lindholt (1999)	10–22% production decline by 2010	
Rosendahl (1996)		Reduction in value of OPEC oil wealth by 33–42%, and non-OPEC oil wealth by 40–54%.
Berg et al. (1997)		Fall of value of OPEC oil wealth by 20%, 8% for non-OPEC.
Donovan et al. (1997)	3.7–5.9% volume reduction by 2010	Notes that limited substitution available in transport.
Ghanem et al. (1998)	17.9% loss of revenue	In trading scenarios.
Bartsch and Müller (2000)	Production decline of 3–5%, revenue fall of 12%	

Source: CEPA (2004), derived from Barker et al. (2001).

types of model has been used to make these estimates, including macro-economic models and specific energy-sector models. Detailed assumptions over, say, the treatment of greenhouse gases other than carbon dioxide and the use of the Kyoto mechanisms also differ between models.

Estimates have been made of the impact of the Kyoto Protocol with and without emissions trading. Table 6.1 sets out a summary of estimated impacts in scenarios which allow for emissions trading. A key feature of these studies is that all show that emissions trading leads to a lower impact on oil production than if trading is not used. Pershing (2000) notes in his review of other studies that none reflect cost mitigation measures that could be taken to lessen the impact, such as the use of sinks, and thus modelled impacts are likely to be overstated. Also, most tend to assume US participation in the market.

A recent study for Statoil by CICERO[3] similarly assumes US participation but is based on a more up-to-date assessment of the EU ETS. In this analysis, oil demand falls by 5–7% below projected levels, but oil prices fall by just 2–3%. Strategic behaviour by OPEC producers to minimize overall impact means that they bear the brunt of the falls in output. Other producers reduce output by 1.6–2.1%, and their revenues fall by 3.5–5%. Notably, all these figures represent reductions below projected increases in revenues as opposed to absolute reductions in income.

What would this mean, realistically, for Russia's oil prices? CEPA (2004) calculate that if the US had participated in the Kyoto Protocol, and assuming this resulted in an oil price decline of about 3% (that is, in line with the CICERO study and consistent with a global demand decline of 6% below projected levels and a price elasticity of 0.5), then Russia's projected oil revenues would fall by 3–5.5%, including both a volume and a price effect.

To examine the impact of alternative scenarios, CEPA (2004) have estimated what the fall in oil demand could be as a proportion of the reduction of demand if the US had participated. This is done by examination of regional and global oil demand (see Table 6.2). A key assumption is that with US involvement oil demand would fall by 1.5–5.5%. Although such impacts are at the low end of those in the published literature, some commentators have observed that high estimates are not plausible as they imply a large reduction (of around 10%) in oil demand by Annex B countries compared with 'business as usual' scenarios.

Table 6.2: Oil and gas demand in Annex B countries

Country	Oil demand		Gas demand	
	% global demand	% of Annex B	% global demand countries	% of Annex B countries
US	25.4	41.4	26.3	36.9
Australia	1.1	1.8	0.9	1.3
EU-15	18.0	29.4	15.2	21.3
Canada	2.5	4.1	3.2	4.5
Japan	6.9	11.3	3.1	4.4
Russia	3.5	5.7	15.3	21.5
Ukraine	0.4	0.7	2.8	3.9
Other Annex B countries	3.5	5.7	4.2	5.9
Total Annex B countries	61.3	100.0	71.2	100.0

Source: BP Statistical Review of World Energy (2003).

Table 6.3 illustrates the impact on Russia's oil revenues under various market conditions. Assuming the EU does not engage in emissions trading, then oil use in other Annex B countries (excluding the US, Australia, Russia and the EU-25) could still be reduced. If OPEC acts as swing producer, Russia would receive lower prices, but on unchanged export volumes. If the EU does engage in emissions trading, then the impact is minimal (-0.03–0%), as domestic oil demand need not be

Table 6.3: Illustrative impact on oil revenues under different levels of participation in the Kyoto Protocol and mechanisms (% per year)

	US out			US in
	EU – no emissions surplus trade	EU – buys emissions surplus	EU does not keep Kyoto commitments	
Russia in	-0.3 – -0.8	-0.03 – 0	N/A	-5.0 – -1.5
Russia out	0	N/A	0.4 – 1.6	-5.0 – -1.5

Source: CEPA (2004).

affected. In contrast, had Russia not ratified and the EU-15 not met its Kyoto commitments, then Russia could have expected a slight increase in oil revenues (0.4–1.6%).

Gas markets

Global gas demand has been rising, partly as a result of increased energy demand, but also as a result of a large increase in the use of this fuel for power generation. This trend is expected to continue. The IEA currently anticipates that global gas consumption will almost double by 2030, although the rate of increase (2.3% per year) will be lower than in the past.[4] Russia's exports are also expected to rise, with growing demand in Europe being the primary driver.[5]

Implementation of the Kyoto Protocol will have two opposing effects on gas demand:

- It is likely to reduce demand for energy and thus potentially that for gas.
- The low carbon content of gas gives the potential for increased demand for gas, as electricity production and other energy use is switched to this fuel, away from coal and oil.

Of these, most market commentators in Europe believe that the second effect (substitution) will dominate. This applies both in the short term (because of the switch to gas in the electricity merit order) and in the long term (as coal/oil power stations are replaced).

The range of estimates for the impact of the Kyoto Protocol on gas markets is wider than those on oil. In Barker et al. (2001), the models surveyed indicate an impact on gas demand ranging from -36.4% to +15%. A modelling study by STATOIL and SNF[6] projects a fall towards the middle of this range, with gas demand declining by 2–3%, and European gas prices dropping by 3%, relative to the scenario without Kyoto.

Table 6.4 shows the analysis by CEPA (2004) of the potential impact of various market scenarios on Russian gas demand. The base case analysis assumes that the EU ETS would have continued even if Russia had not ratified the Kyoto Protocol and the treaty had not come into force. This is reasonable given that the EU ETS is legally binding regardless of the treaty status, but means that the Protocol's entry into force is

Table 6.4: Impact of different levels of participation in the Kyoto Protocol on gas demand

	EU – no emissions surplus trade	EU – emission surplus trade	EU does not keep Kyoto commitments
Russia in	• EU demand no change • Increased Japanese interest in Russian gas • Russia's trading relationship with EU improves	• EU demand – increase in gas demand • Increased Japanese interest in Russian gas • Russia's trading relationship with EU improves	N/A
Russia out	N/A	N/A	• Reduced EU gas demand of 6%–7% compared to status quo because of fuel substitution

Source: CEPA (2004).

likely to have a negligible effect relative to the base case. However, if for some reason the EU ETS did not continue, then there would be a reduction in EU gas demand as presumably there would be less pressure on European industry to reduce emissions.

If the EU were to engage in emissions surplus trading, this would allow an increase in EU energy demand as increases in emissions would be offset by purchases of others' surpluses. Alternatively, increases in demand could be offset by an expansion in the use of gas, in which case Russia could expect slightly higher revenues from gas exports. If the EU were to abandon the EU ETS, energy demand would rise, but the pattern of the fossil fuel demand would change (compared with the base case projection). Assuming the substitution effect dominates, gas demand would fall. Modelling studies by ICF Consulting point to increased electricity production from gas, with an associated increase in gas

demand of 6–7% (the higher figure is associated with the participation of EU accession countries).

More significant changes in Russian gas demand are likely to arise from implementation of the Kyoto Protocol by other Annex B economies to which Russia could sell gas, particularly Japan. The relatively low current demand for gas from Japan means that the impact of the Kyoto Protocol is likely to be small, but positive. However, strategic changes in Japan and pressures to meet its Kyoto target could induce that country to increase its engagement with Russia over investment in gas infrastructure. In this case, the benefits to Russia could be substantial, both financially and strategically. Russia's current dependence on EU markets (the EU buys more than half of Russia's oil and 62% of its gas exports[7]) means that diversification of buyers is likely to be attractive to Russia. It is also possible that Europe would feel more confident that Russia was a secure trading partner, and this would facilitate increased European gas demand.

Ratification decisions will also have an impact on prices. Gas contract prices are mainly linked to oil prices. It is possible that this will change prior to the first commitment period, and that new contracts will be struck with different indexation clauses. As a base case, it assumed that oil-linked pricing will continue.

Strategic behaviour

Russia's own strategic behaviour is likely to influence the impacts of the Kyoto Protocol on the country's energy exports. As noted in Chapter 5, Russia could raise the value of emissions permits now but also, and more significantly, in the future (i.e. nearer 2012) by exercising its monopoly power in the market and restricting supply of its emissions surplus. However, such restrictions could also constrain demand for its fossil fuels.

A number of studies have analysed the possible linkages between sales of surplus emissions and demand for Russia's fossil fuels.[8] These suggest that if Russia restricts its sale of surplus emission permits too much, it will reduce international demand for gas and thus reduce the value of Russia's exports. On the other hand, Hagem et al. (2004) argue there is a two-way link between fossil-fuel and carbon prices and that the combined exercise of market power in emission and gas markets could lead to an increase in gas exports.

These models reinforce the conclusion that there is a very large range

of potential outcomes, depending on the assumptions made about market behaviour. In any case, Russian strategic behaviour in an emissions trading market will only be relevant to the extent that emissions surplus purchases occur.

Overall impact on fossil-fuel export revenues

Modelling studies do indicate that actions to reduce the impact of greenhouse gas emissions will have important effects on energy markets. CEPA's estimates of the overall impact of ratification decisions on Russia's energy export revenues are set out in Table 6.5. Such estimates should be treated with caution, but suggest that assuming the EU keeps its commitments *and* engages in surplus trading, then the overall impact on Russia's energy revenues will be non-existent or minimal. With no emissions trading, Russia's energy revenues could fall slightly – by about US$0.7 billion per year. Were the US to ratify the Kyoto Protocol, Russia's export revenues would fall by a much greater amount – perhaps US$4 billion per year.

Table 6.5: Illustrative annual impact on Russia's energy exports of ratification decisions (US$ billion/year)

	US out			US in
	EU – no emissions surplus trade	EU – buys emissions surplus	EU does not keep Kyoto commitments	
Russia in	-0.7 – -0.2	-0.1 – 0.0	N/A	-4.0 – -1.5
Russia out	0	N/A	-1.0 – 0.1	-4.0 – -1.5
	(Status quo)			

Source: CEPA (2004).

In any case, the revenue impact of greenhouse gas mitigation measures under the Kyoto Protocol is small compared with the volatility inherent in the markets as a result of changing OPEC behaviour and other uncertainties (e.g. when Iraqi oil supplies will be fully restored and how the fragile political and security situation in the Middle East and Venezuela will develop). The IEA estimates that the geopolitical risk

premium alone inherent in the oil price reached $10 per barrel in mid-2004.[9] In addition one needs to take account of the impact of other hazards, such as Hurricane Katrina in August 2005, which sent oil prices soaring. Conversely, there is the possibility of an economic slowdown and reduced energy demand as countries respond to the high prices.[10] Nevertheless strategic changes, such as enhanced Japanese investment in Russia, could be important likely impacts of ratification decisions.

Energy-intensive exports

While implementation of the Kyoto Protocol may negatively affect the overall value of fossil-fuel exports, the impact on Russia's energy-intensive exports is likely to be positive. As Chapter 5 showed, Russia is highly likely to have an emissions surplus in the first commitment period. Thus the marginal cost of emissions arising from activities within Russia will be effectively zero, whereas in other Annex B countries, emissions trading and other measures to constrain emissions are likely to add to the cost of production. This puts Russia at a carbon cost advantage in the production of energy-intensive goods relative to other Annex B countries.

The following section (based largely on CEPA, 2004) outlines factors affecting the value of this cost advantage to Russia and presents estimates of the impact on the value of the aluminium and ferrous metals sectors under various scenarios.

Table 6.6: Value of exports of energy-intensive products (US$ billion, 2003)

	Exports to non-FSU countries	Exports to FSU countries	Total
Metals	16.2	1.2	17.4
Pulp and paper	4.9	0.5	5.4
Total	21.1	1.7	22.8

Source: Russian State Customs Committee 2004, available at *www.customs.ru.*
FSU = Former Soviet Union.

Impacts

Valuing the impact of Russia's carbon cost advantage on exports is not straightforward, because of the numerous factors which will affect each industry. These include the volume, value and embodied carbon content[11] of energy-intensive exports from Russia; differences in the carbon price in other Annex B countries; whether or not a carbon tax is imposed on energy-intensive products; the proportion of production in non-Annex 1 countries, with low carbon prices themselves; and the elasticity of demand and supply. The positive impact is potentially large; Russia's most important energy-intensive exports were valued at US\$22.8 billion in 2003 (see Table 6.6).[12] Some studies have put the annual value of the carbon cost advantage as high as US\$4.9 billion,[13] although this figure seems implausible.

CEPA (2004) have estimated the impact of differing levels of participation in the Kyoto Protocol on two major energy-intensive product groups – aluminium and ferrous metals – which together account for around half of Russia's energy-intensive exports. In valuing the impact for particular products, they have considered the carbon content of exports and the value of that content using an assumption about the difference between Russian carbon prices and those faced by competitors, and assessing the proportion of production that is met by competitors with a higher price for carbon.

Table 6.7: Illustrative impact of different levels of participation in the Kyoto Protocol on the value of Russia's major energy-intensive products (US\$ million)

	EU does not keep Kyoto commitments	EU only	EU, plus Canada and Japan	US plus EU, Canada, Japan
Market conditions	Carbon price low everywhere	Carbon price high in EU, but low elsewhere	Carbon price high in EU, Japan, Canada	Carbon price high in all Annex B countries
Russia in	N/A	N/A	30–90	90–260
Russia out	60–180	Status quo	N/A	90–260

Source: CEPA (2004).

Russia exported around 3 million tonnes of aluminium in 2003, with an estimated embodied carbon dioxide content of 10.5 tonnes per tonne of aluminium.[14] With a value of US\$5–15 per tonne of carbon dioxide, this implies the total carbon value of aluminium exports is US\$150–470 million. Exports of ferrous metals account for a further estimated carbon value of US\$100–290 million. Russia would not keep all this value, as it will still face competition from non-Annex 1 countries which will also incur no extra costs from carbon abatement as they have no targets under the Kyoto Protocol. Adjusting for this on the basis of the proportion of global production in Annex B countries that ratify reduces the value of the carbon cost advantage to Russia and gives the reduced values set out in Table 6.7. There would also be a smaller effect from other products which is probably unlikely to increase these estimates by more than 50%.

CEPA's estimate of the value impact on aluminium and ferrous metal exports is relatively modest, and at a maximum around US\$260 million, even with US participation. Without the US, the carbon cost advantage to Russia of ratification is estimated to be much lower, with a maximum of US\$90 million. Without Russian or EU ratification, however, the value of Russia's energy-intensive exports would have been reduced.

Conclusions

This chapter shows that international action to curb greenhouse gas emissions can have important effects on energy markets and markets for energy-intensive products. Model analyses suggest that while the Kyoto Protocol's entry into force could reduce the overall value of Russia's energy exports, the effect is likely to be small given the withdrawal of the US and can be reduced through emissions trading. On the positive side, it could help forge significant strategic economic links between Russia and, in particular, Japan and Europe. Russia would also benefit from a significant carbon cost advantage over most other Annex B countries for its energy-intensive products.

However, it is important to view the potential impacts of the Kyoto Protocol in the context of wider changes in the energy market as a whole. Most analyses to date (including the CEPA study) were conducted at a time when oil (and gas) prices were significantly lower than today. In the three years 2003–05, oil prices more than doubled, and by late 2005 were on average some four time higher than in the mid-

to late 1990s.[15] These increases were driven by rising consumer demand, security concerns, production and refining capacity constraints and, in September 2005, the fall-out from Hurricanes Katrina and Rita. In a world of static demand, high oil prices are reflected in higher revenues to producer countries. Under these circumstances, the projected gains and losses under the various climate scenarios above would be greater in absolute terms than is indicated in existing studies, but small in relation to the impact of wider changes in the market.

An enduring concern of producer countries is that high prices also provide incentives for changes in consumer behaviour, enhance the competitiveness of non-conventional fossil fuels and alternatives, and bring the risk of an economic slowdown or recession in precisely the markets that producers need – all of which could reduce demand and prices in the medium to longer term. There is already some evidence of this as a result of recent price hikes: US and European consumers are seeking out alternative fuels and/or more efficient cars, and developing-country importers are seeking to curb imports through energy efficiency measures.[16] If high oil prices are sustained, then the effects of such changes in consumer behaviour on oil demand could be greater than any resulting from measures to tackle climate change.

7 JOINT IMPLEMENTATION IN RUSSIA: PROSPECTS AND VALUE

JI is effectively an alternative mechanism for allowing a trade of AAUs. Instead of making a direct purchase, a country gains the units through an investment, and part of the return on that investment accrues in the form of emissions credits that are then offset against the assigned amount of the investing country. As an Annex 1 country, Russia is in theory eligible to host JI projects as long as it complies with the institutional requirements of the Kyoto Protocol (see Chapter 9). Governments may invest directly in JI or via international funds, or they can establish rules so that companies can directly invest in JI projects to buy emission units that can be used to balance emission commitments.

In theory, there is significant potential for JI in Russia. However, other factors such as additionality (see Chapter 4), the feasibility of the project plan and the availability of actual proposals for foreign investors will influence the extent of JI projects in Russia. Therefore, this chapter focuses first on the potential Russian project hosts – the main Russian actors likely to come up with proposals, the types of projects and potential demand-side interest. The chapter also looks at the extent to which JI investments may add to overall FDI.

Supply and demand

Russian project hosts

Russian business appears to have recognized the potential for JI. Indeed, the Dutch governmental JI bidding system ERUPT has received a number of good-quality project proposals from Russia. This is a promising sign, as a supply of projects will be crucial to the development of a JI market in Russia.

Individual Russian companies, notably RAO UES, have spent a great deal of time and resources in preparing potential JI projects. RAO UES

provides 70% of electricity and 32% of heating in Russia, and, significantly, accounts for 30% of the total of Russia's greenhouse gas emissions.[1] Its current project portfolio contains some energy efficiency projects; however, the main focus of the company seems to be on renewable energy, especially on geothermal energy.[2] RAO UES has already created the greenhouse gas inventory necessary for projects and developed professional JI project supply services.

The gas giant Gazprom accounted for some 12.5% of Russia's total greenhouse gas emissions in 2000. The company has undertaken some pilot projects with the German Ruhrgas, and one project with a consortium of Japanese companies, involving replacement of pipes and compressors and installation of additional looping in the supply system.[3] Since Gazprom is the main actor in the gas industry, the company is the potential host of most gas sector projects. The company is planning to attract JI investments to upgrade its infrastructure[4] and has drawn up a greenhouse gas inventory. To date Gazprom's approach has been to cooperate with existing partners instead of looking for new investors by establishing a JI facility.[5]

A number of other smaller actors are actively seeking to participate in the emerging carbon markets. Some, such as OJSC Kotlas Pulp and Paper Mill, have submitted project proposals to international tenders, e.g. the World Bank. In northwestern Russia, the local energy-saving companies have portfolios of projects which were typical of the pilot phase, such as switching small boiler houses from coal to local biomass and improving the efficiency of buildings. The Moscow-based National Carbon Sequestration Foundation has also submitted proposals to government tender programmes. The JI Committee is also seeking to facilitate JI projects in Russia, but so far this private consultancy has announced no firm project deals.

A number of industries and groups of companies have been actively lobbying the Russian government on Kyoto market issues. The most prominent of these is the National Carbon Union (NCU) whose members include RAO UES, the Ministry of Transport, RusAl and MDM Bank. In 2003 a number of the largest Russian corporations began to coordinate their activity through a special working group of the Economic Department of the President of the Russian Federation. Significantly, the members of the Union are interested in the early creation of a Russian emission allowances market and are prepared to bear the costs related to its formation. These may include:

- greenhouse gas inventories by market participants;
- establishing corporate and national systems of monitoring;
- registration, certification and verification of greenhouse gas emissions reductions; and
- arranging special trade areas.[6]

This high level of interest in JI from prospective project hosts and their growing experience on government tender programmes are encouraging, but ultimately there also need to be companies and governments willing to invest in Russia.

Investor interest

In the absence of the US the demand for JI projects will be led by the EU, Japan and Canada (see Chapter 4). These potential investors can be divided into two groups: government-led programmes and private-sector investors. The former are popular in the EU, although the private-sector approach is favoured in Japan and Canada. An additional form of JI activity management is investing in an international fund such as the Prototype Carbon Fund (PCF) of the World Bank.

The strength of the EU's demand will depend on both the level of member states' public procurement and the demand from operators under the EU Emissions Trading Scheme (EU ETS). A number of EU governments have established or are in the process of establishing funds to invest in JI and CDM projects, which provide some demand opportunities. The situation is less clear in Japan and Canada, although both will probably need to turn to the international markets in order to comply with the Kyoto Protocol. So far, neither of them has a governmental purchasing programme and the focus is on action via private-sector actors. Japanese demand for Russian credits is likely to depend in part on political relations between the two countries and the Japanese desire to enhance cooperation over energy supplies. Japanese actors are likely to be less interested in the more bureaucratic Track 2 JI projects, given their experiences of the CDM bureaucracy. Japanese companies have implemented some feasibility studies in Russia, although most of these studies have not yet been developed to projects.[7] There have been reports of a project with Japanese companies (see Box 7.1 below) and of Toyota Tsusho's cooperation with RAO UES Rossii Energy Carbon Facility.[8] However, the exact status of these projects

remains unclear. The Canadian government also aims to facilitate JI activities by private-sector actors.[9] A similar range of climatic conditions means that Canadian expertise could be very valuable to Russia as it seeks to modernize its ageing infrastructure.[10]

The first public fund to invest in climate change projects was the Prototype Carbon Fund (PCF) of the World Bank. Since its establishment in 1999, several other funds have been opened by the World Bank Carbon Finance Unit. Many governments have already invested in these funds, often as an additional activity to their domestic JI programmes. The Netherlands, Italy and Denmark have also established national funds hosted by the World Bank, and a number of governments and private companies have invested in PCF's focused funds such as the BioCarbon Fund (BCF) and Community Development Carbon Fund (CDCF). Many large private-sector actors have invested in the public funds. Russia is not one of the host countries that have signed a Memorandum of Understanding with the World Bank Carbon Funds. However, the Carbon Finance Unit of the Bank reports that it is possible for the Funds to be applied to JI projects in Russia if the government provides a Letter of Endorsement and a Letter of Approval by the Minister of Economy after the project is prepared.

Other similar funds of relevance to Russia include the Baltic Sea Region Testing Ground Facility (TGF) established by the governments of the Nordic countries and hosted by the Nordic Environment Finance Corporation (NEFCO). Under this fund, the project identification process is continuous (as opposed to there being a tender system) and in early 2005 some Russian projects had already received preliminary acceptance and were awaiting final approval. However, Russia has not signed the TGF agreement and this may undermine the prospects for success under this programme.

Table 7.1 summarizes the preparations of EU countries, Japan and Canada for JI projects relevant to Russia. Among the biggest potential investors interested in Russian JI projects are the Dutch government programmes. The Dutch ERUPT 3 tender programme in 2003 had a number of project applications from Russia; however, these lacked the required Letter of Approval from the Russian government as no decision had yet been reached on ratification of the Protocol. ERUPT 4 received 14 expressions of interest from Russia, and the prospective hosts of seven of these were invited to submit a formal proposal. Five proposals were

Table 7.1: JI activities relevant to Russia (by country)

Country	Details	Approach to Russia
The Netherlands	The Netherlands ERUPT bidding programme is open to all eligible JI host countries. The current ERUPT tender procedure is the fifth, and has attracted some Russian proposals. The Netherlands has set up a new Carbon Fund to invest in JI emission reduction projects in central and eastern Europe together with the EBRD. It also participates in the PCF and CDCF.	The Netherlands government has a special interest in – and wide pilot experience of – Russian projects. It signed Memoranda of Interest with three Russian regions – Omsk, Vologda and Kostroma – in September 2003, and is keen to accommodate Russian projects through ERUPT.
Italy	The Italian government established a Carbon Fund in 2003 together with the World Bank. The fund accepts both JI and CDM projects; however, no Russian projects have been accepted so far. Italy has also invested in the BCF and CDCF.	Italy has announced a specific tender programme for Russian projects, focusing mostly on energy efficiency projects. It has also established cooperation with the JI Committee.
Austria	Austria's second JI tender programme opened in October 2004. Austria has also invested in CDCF.	No Russian projects so far, but interested in Russian projects in the future.
Finland	The Finnish government has identified over 50 potential JI projects in transition countries. In addition, the country has invested in the PCF and the TGF.	Finland has previously sought Russian projects which failed because the Russian government did not sign a Letter of Intent.

Sweden	Sweden ran a SICLIP JI tender in 2003, and is currently preparing the next funding round. The country has invested in the TGF and PCF.	Experience and good contacts with Russian project hosts. Some Russian proposals included in the 2003 tender, but not successful. Future JI activities likely to focus more on Russia. Negotiating on bilateral agreement with Russia. Also bio-energy-related cooperation with Russia, which might facilitate JI projects.
Norway	Invested in the PCF and TGF.	
Denmark	Denmark has two governmental funds, one managed by a government agency and a Carbon Facility hosted by Ecosecurities. Invested in the TGF.	Denmark has had a special interest in Russian projects, and accepted some RAO UES projects in 2004.
Germany	A German bank, KfW, and the German federal government opened a Carbon Fund to invest in JI and CDM projects. Germany has also recently joined the TGF.	Ruhrgas has implemented pilot projects with Gazprom. Cooperation planned to continue, and there are plans for JI projects. The German government has established cooperation with JI Committee which has submitted 10 project proposals for review.
Canada	Canada has invested in the PCF, BCF and CDCF. There is no national JI/CDM investment fund but a facilitation programme exists for private investments by Canadian companies.	Some interest expressed but no known Russian projects.
Japan	Japanese companies established a greenhouse gas Reduction Fund in 2004. Several private companies have invested in the Japanese fund and various World Bank carbon funds.	Japanese companies have done some feasibility studies in Russia, but the attitude towards Russian JI projects is very cautious. One Japanese-Russian project has been reported by Gazprom.

Sources: Communications with governmental programmes, websites of governmental programmes and funds.

submitted, but again they had to be turned down owing to the lack of a Letter of Approval. ERUPT 5 invited two Russian project hosts to submit a full proposal, and one project has made it to the public comments phase. This project has a Letter of Endorsement signed by Roshydromet, but according to the Dutch programme office the Russian government has not issued the vital Letters of Approval. In May 2005, the Danish government made a preliminary choice of two Russian projects but again did not receive Letters of Approval. In addition, the German government is looking at a project portfolio in Russia.[11]

Most investor interest to date has come from governmental investors but there is also evidence of interest from private-sector buyers and, in particular, large companies in countries that have no government JI programmes such as Canada and Japan. Some examples are given in Boxes 7.1 and 7.2.

Potential for Russian JI projects

Project types

Table 7.2 provides a generic list of JI project types per sector. Evidence from the pilot AIJ phase (see Chapter 8) suggests that the largest practical

---

Box 7.1: Japanese industry's interest in Russian JI projects: Nippon Steel Company and the Sumitomo Commercial Investments Corporation

Nippon Steel Company and the Sumitomo Commercial Investments Corporation are considering US$283 million of JI investments to repair and modernize some Gazprom pipelines in Russia. The preliminary studies carried out indicate that greenhouse gas emissions could be reduced by as much as 5 $MtCO_2e$, the equivalent of up to 8% of the annual emissions of the Nippon Steel Company, and almost 1% of total emissions from Japanese industry.

Source: 'Japanese firms consider JI investment in Gazprom pipelines', *Point Carbon*, 2 February 2004. Available at *http://www.pointcarbon.com/ article.php? articleID=3169&categoryID=147*.

> **Box 7.2: German industry's interest in Russian JI projects:**
> **Ruhrgas**
>
> During a carbon business forum at the Moscow climate conference in September 2003, the German gas supply firm Ruhrgas announced plans to further extend its financing of a Russian gas pipeline overhaul programme. This is expected to cut emissions equivalent to 5 $MtCO_2$ per year by 2007. In addition to the value of the investments, Russia would benefit from resource savings, an increase in export potential and the modernization of its infrastructure. Cooperation between Gazprom and Ruhrgas AG includes the optimization of gas transmission operations in Russia. Expert help in solving technological problems will result in a significant reduction of gas consumption by compressor station drive systems, and a consequent reduction of CO_2 emissions. This is the aim of the two companies' first large JI project.
>
> *Sources:* 'EU companies looking east for Kyoto credits', *Point Carbon*, 29 October 2003. Available at *http://www.pointcarbon.com/article. php?articleID =2181*; 'Partners of Gazprom: Ruhrgas', *http://www.Gazprom.ru/eng/articles/ article8925.shtml*, accessed 25 July 2005.

potential of Russian projects probably lies in fuel switching and in energy efficiency improvements within the energy, industrial and residential/ public sectors. According to Mielke et al.,[12] the majority of JI projects are likely to focus on investments in new power generation equipment, reductions in gas losses during transmission, reduction of gas flaring/ venting in the oil sector and energy efficiency investments. However, JI activities in the oil and gas sector would require an initiative by Russian actors which has been absent so far.

Russia has a significant renewable energy potential and projects geared to realizing this potential could be eligible under JI. The IEA especially has emphasized the potential of fuel switching from coal to renewables: for solar water heating systems to replace or supplement conventional district heating boilers and for wind power to replace or supplement diesel generators in isolated settlements.[13] However, at

Table 7.2: Generic list of potential JI project types per sector

Sector	Project types
Energy sector	
Power	Combined cycle gas turbines, distributive networks, clean coal technologies
	Fuel switching
Oil & gas	Reduction in gas flaring and venting
	Reduction in gas leakage in transmission, compressor upgrades
	Oil refining: retrofit, CHP
Renewable energy	Wind, solar, biomass, hydro, geothermal, fuel cells
Energy efficiency	Equipment modernization, design, processes or end-use
Industrial sector	
Energy efficiency	Boilers, motors, lighting, CHP
Chemicals, paper, metallurgy	Retrofit, replacing obsolete equipment
Iron and steel	Production processes
Waste fuel recovery	Cement sector, methane capture from landfills
Residential/public sector	
Buildings	Insulation, improving roofs, double glazing, energy metering
Heating systems	Insulation of pipelines, optimization of pump systems
	Efficiency of combustion
	Fuel switching
Forestry sector	
Land use change	Reforestation

Source: Based on Mielke et al. (2004).

current domestic energy prices, it is doubtful that renewable energy projects could compete with fossil fuels in Russia.[14] The one possible exception is biomass. There is a large potential to switch to local biomass in many northern regions of Russia as many have forestry industrial complexes which could readily increase the utilization of waste wood in energy production. A further attraction is that potential Russian hosts often have existing expertise in such projects.

Very significant JI project potential also exists in the oil and gas sector,

particularly through projects aimed at cutting the amount of associate gas flared in oil production or insulating old leaking gas pipelines. The Gazprom website lists a range of energy-saving measures, including the optimization of transmission system gas flow, replacement of gas compressor units, implementation of automated control systems and replacement of boilers.[15]

Scope of JI in Russia

The scope for JI in Russia derives from the imperative to modernize the country's ageing energy infrastructure and the associated investment required. The investment needs of the Russian energy sector are enormous: the IEA estimates that US$934 billion will be needed to underpin the projected growth in energy supply from 2003 to 2030.[16] The Russian Ministry of Industry and Energy similarly estimates Russia's investment requirements to be some US$660–810 billion over the period 2001–20, and US$260–300 billion up to 2010.[17]

Projections of investment needs, by sector, are shown in Figure 7.1.[18] All three major sectors – oil, gas and electricity – demand significant shares. Investment requirements in coal and heat supply are modest in comparison, while investment in energy efficiency is a potential growth industry. Under current investment patterns, it is unclear how these needs will be met. Only 13% of total investment in the energy sector originates from outside Russia; of that, 95% goes to the oil industry. There is minimal FDI in the electricity and other industry sectors.[19]

At this stage it is difficult to say what proportion of future investment needs will be met through JI. To date, JI project agreements have been relatively small, and the received wisdom appears to be that JI could therefore account for only a relatively small proportion of investment needs. This said, there is no inherent reason why a larger proportion could not be defined as JI, as much investment in gas and electricity infrastructure will entail significant, identifiable, associated emission reductions. Whether or not these JI investments materialize, and their magnitude, will depend on a number of factors, including:

- How quickly and effectively Russia meets the Kyoto compliance and monitoring requirements, including whether international verification will be needed for monitoring ERUs (Track 2) and the magnitude of transaction costs involved in this process.

Figure 7.1: Russia's energy industry investment needs (US$ billion)

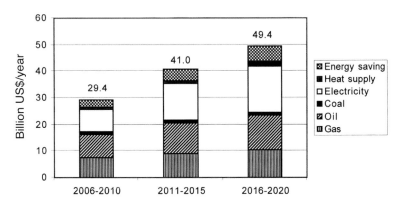

Source: Pluzhnikov (2003).

- The pace and depth of reforms in the energy sector and the enabling environment in general.
- Any instruments and mechanisms that investing governments are prepared to introduce to make JI more acceptable and feasible for their industries.
- The price of allowances under the EU ETS, whether Canada and Japan establish trading systems and whether these are linked to the EU ETS.
- National Allocation Plans of the new EU member states under the EU ETS, which will determine the proportion of surplus emissions that can be traded under the EU ETS. An anticipated emissions surplus in, say, Poland means that the Polish government may be tempted to give its companies over-generous allocations well beyond anticipated requirements – a practice the European Commission is keen to avoid.
- The growth of the CDM market and its ability to satisfy the demand for emission credits.
- Levels of investment from the United States and other non-Kyoto signatories in Russia and the extent to which this may crowd out investment through JI, particularly in the light of its potentially cumbersome bureaucratic procedures.

Russian sources indicate that a total of US$1–2 billion could be invested in carbon projects. [20] This may be over-conservative given the size of investment needed in the Russian energy and energy-intensive industries and the fact that much of this could theoretically come under JI. Thus CEPA (2004) suggest that an indicative maximum for JI investments of US$5 billion over the first commitment period is plausible. Even so, this amounts to only a small proportion (2%) of overall investment requirements.

Value of JI

The direct benefit of JI to Russia will depend on the extent to which it is investment that would not otherwise have taken place. Projects selected for JI would be different from those undertaken by Russian industry on its own account as the priority would be on emissions reductions rather than economic value. This means that JI is unlikely to crowd out other planned investment.

An indirect benefit of JI – and Russia's decision to ratify the Kyoto Protocol in general – is that it could speed up the ongoing reform programmes for the energy sector. In particular, compliance responsibilities under the Protocol would positively support reforms aimed at greater transparency in the energy sector and better reporting and monitoring capability. Moreover, greater integration of the Russian energy sector with those of other countries, and economic and technical cooperation to cut greenhouse gases, could be sources of valuable capacity-building and learning which might speed up the restructuring process. In general, however, these are fairly weak links and, in practice, the pace of reform and improvements in the enabling environment are far more dependent on high-level political will and the relationship between the Kremlin and energy-sector participants.

A key issue for both the Russian government and industry is whether the Kyoto mechanisms – and notably JI – will deliver any additional FDI that would not otherwise have taken place. There are two reasons why it may:

- Private investors will not only enhance their established links with Russian hosts, but as they develop the infrastructure within their companies to undertake projects, they are likely to find further opportunities.

- The reforms and changes to the legal framework necessary to accommodate substantial JI investment could improve the general investment climate.

How big these knock-on effects may be is uncertain. CEPA (2004) suggest that this incremental FDI could yield an indicative maximum of US$5 billion of investment (on top of the potential US$5 billion of JI

Table 7.3: Possible positive impacts and constraints of JI on FDI to Russia

Possible positive impacts of JI on FDI	Possible constraints of JI as an FDI lever
<ul><li>A positive price on EU ETS for greenhouse gas permits achieved via JI will enhance the commercial returns on investment project.</li><li>Involvement of both Russian and investing firm's governments in the transaction improves the risk profile of the project.</li><li>Apart from Ukraine, Russia has one of the lowest greenhouse gas abatement costs of Annex 1 countries.</li><li>The Russian government may be more supportive of JI than other investment as: (i) JI investment is specifically aimed at modernizing the processes and equipment of Russian industries; and (ii) greater greenhouse gas allowances on the EU and other markets will stimulate demand for Russian fossil fuels.</li></ul>	<ul><li>Increased bureaucracy, such as ensuring additionality, verification and certification of emissions, related to implementing a JI project may hinder growth of investment.</li><li>Difficulties and transaction costs involved in calculating BaU emissions scenarios could reduce investor interest.</li><li>Verification requirements for Track 2 projects, in particular, could also limit interest.</li><li>Additional risks involved for investors are: the yield of ERU, the price level of ERU on the EU ETS/worldwide, and the effects of negotiations related to the next commitment period.</li></ul>

Source: CEPA (2004).

investments indicated earlier). These figures reflect a combination of CEPA's own assessment and estimates by the NCU in Russia. If the creation of the JI process does contribute to wider reforms then the economic benefit could be far larger.

While JI may in general have a positive impact on FDI, there are some constraints. Table 7.3 summarizes the overall picture.

The incremental investment generated by JI will have benefits over and above the investment itself. The value of this can be approximated using a Keynesian multiplier which CEPA (2004) judge to be in the range 1.3–1.7. This gives a net value of 0.3–0.7 multiplied by the investment made. CEPA (2004) estimate that JI investment for the first commitment period without the United States could be in the range US$1–5 billion in total, with an additional US$1–5 billion of non-JI FDI. CEPA further estimate that this investment would have a value of US$0.1–1.4 billion for each year in the first commitment period.

Unsurprisingly, the incremental benefit of JI to Russia would be higher if the United States were to participate in the Kyoto Protocol. With the US, the additional benefit to Russia of JI over the Kyoto first commitment period could have been US$1.5–7.5 billion, with an annual benefit of US$0.2–2.1 billion. While these figures must be treated with caution, they do illustrate both the order of magnitude of the value of JI to Russia and the impact of the US withdrawal.

Conclusions

The potential scope for JI in Russia is huge, especially for investments in fuel switching and energy efficiency improvement projects. Moreover, JI could probably facilitate FDI because it would also help companies to find other investment projects. By late 2005, however, no Russian JI projects had been implemented because the Russian government had not provided the required Letters of Approval to potential investors. In the past, this may have been due in part to Russia's indecision over whether to ratify the Kyoto Protocol. With the Protocol now in force, Russia will need to move swiftly if it is to realize the potential for JI.

8 LESSONS LEARNT FROM AIJ PILOT PROJECTS

This chapter focuses on lessons learnt from implementation of projects under the Activities Implemented Jointly (AIJ) phase in Russia. The AIJ pilot phase was established to gain experience for the future project mechanisms. The UNFCCC's First Conference of Parties (COP-1), held in Berlin in 1995, established the pilot phase of the project-based Kyoto mechanisms.[1] Under the pilot phase there is no crediting of the emission reductions generated, and the prime advantage to investors was in gaining experience for future projects. The chapter highlights the problems foreign investors experienced when implementing pilot projects in Russia over the period of 1995–2001 and what these mean for the success of joint implementation (JI) projects in the future.

Russian domestic administration

The Russian government established the Interagency Commission on Climate Change, 'the Commission', in 1994 to bear the main responsibility for both international and domestic climate policy, including approval of projects. The leading agency was the Russian Federal Service for Hydrometeorology and Environmental Monitoring (Roshydromet), which acted as the chair of the Commission. The Ministry of Economic Development and Trade was introduced as a co-chair of the Commission in 1999 and it took over the leadership role in Russian climate policy in 2002.[2]

The Russian national project approval system was established to facilitate pilot activities. Roshydromet established a joint implementation office and the Commission was responsible for the approval of the projects. A foreign investor required a Letter of Intent signed by Roshydromet and approval by the Commission in order to register a project under the UNFCCC.[3]

COP-1 introduced criteria for AIJ projects. The Commission further defined the main criteria for AIJ pilot projects in Russia as follows:

- Projects should be additional to 'non-regret' measures or business as usual and aim at reducing greenhouse gas emissions or enhancing carbon sinks.
- Projects should be voluntary for both investor and host.
- Results of projects should be verified and reviewed by the Commission.
- Projects should be related to investments.
- Parties should stimulate private-sector actors to JI activities.
- Documents have to be presented to the Commission in Russian.[4]

Projects implemented in Russia

Russia hosted a number of pilot phase projects but not all of them were registered under the AIJ pilot programme. There were nine official pilot projects and some 25 similar projects implemented outside the official pilot phase.[5] Both categories of projects in Russia appeared on the leading agency's website.[6] Only a few investor countries implemented or planned to implement pilot projects in Russia. Three investor countries – Germany, the Netherlands and United States – registered Russian projects under the official pilot phase. Sweden and Finland implemented or planned to undertake Russian projects, but did not register them under the pilot programme. In addition to registered projects, both the Netherlands and the United States also had projects or project plans outside the official pilot phase.

Most pilot projects in Russia focused on the energy sector and as such included elements of energy efficiency (11), fuel switching (9) or energy saving (6).[7] Some projects were a combination of two or more project types, and five unregistered projects did not report any specific project type owing to their failure at an early stage. Table 8.1 illustrates the distribution of project types.

The failure level for pilot projects in Russia was high. Nine of the projects involved were either cancelled or delayed; 17 were completed. There was no information available concerning the status of two of the unregistered projects. Only one project was officially in the process of

Table 8.1: Distribution of pilot projects by activity

	Energy efficiency	Energy saving	Fuel switching	Fugitive gas capture	Forestry
Registered	2	1	1	2	1
Unregistered	9	5	8	–	–
TOTAL	11	6	9	2	1

Table 8.2: Implementation status of projects

	Completed	In progress	Cancelled or delayed	No information
Registered	3	–	3	–
Unregistered	14	1	6	2
TOTAL	17	1	9	2

implementation. Table 8.2 summarizes the status of the projects. For further details on the projects involved in this study, see Appendix 1.

Problems experienced

Institutional problems

The initial, and most critical, set of problems with official pilot projects in Russia is related to institutional structures. About half (53%) of the problems experienced can be categorized as institutional. These contributed to most of the project failures at an early stage – six of the nine cancelled or delayed projects.

The institutional structure of the Russian administration caused significant problems with regard to project approval. Roshydromet experienced problems over its authority to coordinate the agencies involved in the Commission.[8] Various Russian actors involved in climate policy expressed a distrust of Roshydromet, and speculated that the agency's employees might have vested interests in accruing personal benefits.[9] Since Roshydromet's expertise is scientific rather than political

or administrative, the agency was not well equipped to manage industrial projects such as pilot project activities.

Project approval and registration with the domestic administration constituted one of the most significant bottlenecks in implementing projects in Russia. The registration process was slow because the Commission failed to organize its biannual meetings. The unclear division of responsibilities between Russian agencies confused foreign investors, who were unsure which agency was responsible for project approval. Investors were aware that only Roshydromet could register projects, but not which of the various Russian agencies could advance registration and approve their project. The significance of this problem is reflected in the fact that over two-thirds of projects were implemented outside the official pilot phase.

Roshydromet charged some US$5,000 to approve a project. Investors expressed concerns about corruption, believing that the funds were being diverted for the personal use of the agency's employees. Some investors argued that paying for the registration of projects would be acceptable if the payment was transparently used to fund the activities of the agency.

Ongoing reforms to Russian legislation also created difficulties with project implementation: since the early 1990s the old Soviet and new Russian legislations have overlapped. Legislative muddles accounted for more than one-fifth of the problems reported with AIJ projects. Russian customs procedures also led to delays and entailed additional costs for project investors. According to Russian certification rules, imported foreign equipment must be separately certified by the relevant Russian authorities, as was the case for pilot projects lacking Roshydromet's approval. This problem was greatest for projects implemented outside the official pilot programme. The lack of a clearly established Value Added Tax scheme and fee structure also caused delays as fees had to be negotiated on a case-by-case basis. Changes in local administration after elections also represented a risk to projects, as newly elected local administrations did not always take over the commitments of the previous regime. In addition, property rights were poorly defined and enforced in Russia.

The institutional requirements of investing governments with regard to pilot projects also acted as barriers to implementation in some cases. Most investing governments required the signature of a Memorandum of Understanding, a bilateral framework agreement. Some investors

regarded the lack of such an agreement as a barrier to project approval. Problems of this nature affected more than 40% of projects studied. Signing a framework agreement was not a straightforward task for Russian governmental actors owing to the general confusion over administrative responsibilities. The lack of clarity over which agency would be entitled to transfer emission reduction credits made it impossible for Russian agencies to sign a Memorandum of Understanding aiming at transfer of credits. By February 2005, none of the governments investing in pilot projects in Russia had signed a government-level framework agreement with Russia, despite the application of political pressure such as bilateral ministerial meetings. This institutional problem caused some investor countries to cease their pilot activities.

Implementation-level problems

Foreign investors experienced various types of problems while working in the field establishing and implementing projects. About one-third of the difficulties experienced occurred during this practical implementation phase.

Finding Russian partners committed to project implementation throughout the project cycle seems to have been a recurring problem. Lack of commitment caused some one-third of project failures. Various Russian actors approached potential investors with project proposals. However, investors were keen to develop their own projects instead of accepting the projects suggested. In some cases the involvement of regional administrations supported both the approval process and implementation of the project by decreasing the bureaucratic burden and thus saving time in negotiations. Occasionally, regional authorities have also been able to put pressure on federal authorities to approve a project. Continuous partnerships with Russian actors are important. This is because the Russian tradition is heavily dependent on personal networks. Even changing an individual employee may put a project at risk. Investors developed pilot programmes on the basis of existing relations, and some regarded continuity of relations as the main strategy to successful project implementation. Almost one-quarter of project participants encountered some problems with their Russian partners.

A related issue is the difficulty in finding Russian partners with the technical and managerial skills required for project implementation. In some cases, investors trained these local-level actors in order to support

project management but were frustrated by the rapid turnover of technically trained staff. Almost half of the projects reported problems of this type. Local infrastructure and material quality can be poor in Russia. Pilot project investors experienced failures with energy equipment and computers. Poor material quality, such as dirty water or low-grade bio fuel, caused extra expenses to projects, as did defective postal services and telephone connections. Half of the projects suffered from problems related to local infrastructure, although these did not cause project failures.

Funding-related problems

A key issue has been the availability of funding for pilot projects which do not generate emission credits – the main incentive to investment in projects under the Kyoto Protocol. This problem was exacerbated by the uncertainty over whether and when the Kyoto Protocol would come into force. This in turn decreased the incentive to get prepared by implementing pilot projects.

Public funding for pilot projects was made available by many governments. These projects were the most successful ones, while programmes based on private-sector funding were more vulnerable to the lack of investment incentives. Some projects were cancelled as a result. It was also very difficult to find local co-funding in Russia and most pilot projects were entirely funded by foreign investors. Many investors considered the lack of local co-funding to be a potential disincentive for the hosts to commit themselves to finalizing the project. Some investors addressed this problem by decreasing their share of total funding. More than half of the projects reported a problem related to availability of funding, and 20% of the cancelled or delayed projects reported a lack of funding and/or local economic support.

Transaction costs associated with project development were also a problem. These cover the wide range of expenses that may be incurred in implementing a project. Dudek and Wiener[10] have divided transaction costs related to JI into six categories: search costs, negotiation costs, approval costs, monitoring costs, enforcement costs and insurance costs. Transaction costs are typically high in Russia owing to the malfunctioning of the economy, infrastructure and administrative system. Some 90% of the projects reported problems which could have led to additional transaction costs including delays with negotiations, importing equipment and loan payments, additional customs fees, infrastructure failures,

etc. Risks to the economic integrity of a project are high because of these unexpected costs and delays.

A more general issue has been the poor investment climate. The investment climate is determined by the functionality of economic institutions, the state of the national economy and practical banking and other relevant business services. At the time of the pilot projects, the investment climate of Russia was widely regarded as unfavourable.[11] This caused problems for about one-third of the projects and contributed to the financial instability of project hosts. Consequently, hardly any local investments were available. For instance, a failure to collect payments from customers delayed some project hosts' repayment of loans to investors. Cash payments, widely in use in Russia instead of bank transfers, also caused problems for foreign investors.

Comparison of project categories

Some differences between the extent of problems faced under the two project categories, registered and unregistered, can be observed:

- Officially registered pilot projects experienced fewer problems in total and fewer categories of problems than unregistered projects.
- Official projects suffered somewhat more from problems with practical implementation problems than unregistered ones.
- Registered projects did not report any problems related to infra-structure and material quality or local expertise and staff, although this may reflect the reporting practices of different sources of information rather than differences of experience.
- Official projects reported more problems related to funding than other projects but this could be because it is easier not to report a failed unregistered project, while the registered projects remain in the UNFCCC database.

The connection between lack of registration and the Russian dysfunctional institutional system is obvious. Table 8.3 shows the subcategories created and the number of projects that have experienced problems in each of the subcategories discussed above.

Table 8.3: Number of projects experiencing problems, by category

	Problem type	Total registered	Unregistered
Institutional			
Institutional structure	26	3	23
Legislation	24	4	20
Requirements of investors	12	3	9
Implementation			
Local infrastructure, material quality	14	0	14
Implementation-level cooperation	7	2	5
Local expertise and staff	14	0	14
Funding-related			
Lack of funding and local economic support	13	4	9
Investment climate unfavourable	10	3	7

Source: Korppoo (2005).

Lessons for Joint Implementation

The pilot project programme has ceased to exist in practice with the approach of the first Kyoto commitment period in 2008. More recent projects are aiming to be recognized as JI projects, since emission reductions will carry an economic value. Even so, there are many lessons to be drawn from past experience of pilot projects. These will need to be addressed if JI projects are to prove more successful.

Lessons from institutional problems:

- The institutional structure of the Russian climate change administration needs to be revisited as the past system was not functional and did not facilitate pilot projects.
- The division of responsibilities between domestic actors needs to be clarified. This was one of the main barriers in the pilot phase, as it made projects in Russia commercially unattractive.
- The lack of clarity concerning the roles of Russian regional authorities and the private sector needs to be addressed if it is not to cause serious complications for future projects.

- On the plus side, future projects are likely to experience fewer problems with the legislative system and the rule of law as they will have to be officially registered in order to produce credits.
- More serious efforts at establishing framework agreements for bilateral cooperation will be required as investors' project criteria for JI projects are likely to be stricter than for pilot projects.

Lessons from implementation-level problems:

- The lack of Russian partners committed to project implementation is likely to continue to limit the number of projects, although economic growth is likely to generate an increased number of actors capable of fulfilling the criteria of foreign investors.
- If the economic development continues towards a market economy system, Russian actors are also more likely to make longer-term commitments in the future. As they gain experience of market economy practices, managerial problems are likely to diminish.
- Problems with the inadequacy or lack of local technical infrastructure and poor material quality may be addressed in part through more careful feasibility studies and selective criteria.

Lessons from funding-related problems:

- High transaction costs seem likely to remain a problem until the economic and legislative problems are completely resolved.
- The requirement of local co-funding is likely to gain importance, partly because investors experienced commitment problems with Russian hosts during the pilot phase.
- The unfavourable investment climate will continue to influence future projects in Russia. However, according to the EBRD,[12] the Russian investment climate is gradually improving in terms of financial, legislative and crime indicators.
- Risks with the economic integrity of Russian projects remain high. Again, stricter criteria for project approval will ensure the most competitive Russian projects are picked and reduce transaction costs relative to those of the pilot projects.

In summary, institutional problems, in particular, need to be resolved if they are not to significantly complicate the implementation of JI projects in Russia. Addressing implementation-level problems will also

be important although many of them can be avoided through better feasibility studies. Of all the problems, funding is likely to be the least relevant in future as the emerging carbon markets will put a price on carbon – a factor largely missing from the pilot phase.

New challenges for Joint Implementation

Russia's economy and administrative system have experienced significant changes since the pilot project programme began in 1995. As discussed in Chapter 2, the economy experienced a serious slump between the early 1990s and 1998, but has grown year on year since then. Future growth prospects are enhanced by recent reforms, whereby many economic structures typical of the market economy have taken over the unclear practices of the transition economy. While there remains a lot to be done before Russia's economy fulfils the criteria of a market economy, past and ongoing reforms mean that future projects will be implemented in a different environment from that in which the pilot projects were operating in the 1990s.

The most significant difference is that, unlike the pilot projects, future projects will be entitled to issue credits that carry economic value against the emission reductions generated. As a result, they will be much more attractive to private-sector funders. Add to this the driver of the EU ETS and it is plausible that there will be a tendency towards more private-sector-funded than government-funded projects. Even so, governmental funding is likely to remain important in the early stages of the Kyoto market as Russian conditions entail a constant risk of instability.

Future projects will face more competition from other project providers in the emerging carbon markets than projects under the pilot phase. Any additional expenses will add to the costs of the credits generated and thus investors will be more careful over transaction costs. Moreover, funding issues are likely to become relevant at an earlier stage of the project cycle as economic factors will be evaluated more carefully.

The market is also becoming more reactive on the investor side and proactive on the host side. Bidding-based project selection systems introduce stricter requirements. These could effectively rule out projects in certain host countries on grounds of cost and/or the preparedness of the country. Thus, the imperative will be for host countries to get their act in order if they are to be considered seriously as prospective partners.

Table 8.4: Summary of problems identified for future projects in Russia

Problem	Status	Description	Importance
Project registration and approval procedure not functional	Unchanged	Various attempts to clarify the situation, in practice remains unclear how to approve a project	High
Ownership of allowances and credits not defined	Unchanged	The Kyoto market makes the ownership of allowances and credits relevant. Main interest groups are private-sector and regions.	Mid
Local implementation environment	Developed	Gradual improvement of conditions. More detailed feasibility studies may prevent some of these problems in the future.	Low
Transaction costs of projects high	Developed	Investors likely to be more careful with additional costs in competitive market. Some improvements with legal and economic reforms. Mandatory registration of projects may reduce transaction costs.	Low
Lack of local funding	Developed	Future investors likely to require local co-funding. Some positive legal developments and some actors willing to co-fund.	Mid
Unfavourable investment climate in Russia	Developed	Unfinished economic reform, but gradually improving. Some positive developments in legislation and enforcement of the rule of law.	Mid
Competitive Kyoto market	New	Greater supply than demand in Kyoto market leads to competition between supplier countries and various mechanisms.	High
Lack of functional compliance institutions	New	Without achieving full compliance Russia can potentially host no projects or Track 2 projects only.	High

Overall, Russian projects will experience more competition in the international carbon market than the pilot projects did. In general, the market price generated by the supply of other joint implementation projects, CDM projects, credits available in the international emissions trading market and domestic measures of investing countries will affect the competitiveness of Russian projects. The pilot phase, by contrast, was rather an exploration of opportunities by government-funded investors.

In the market of greater supply than demand, credits generated by JI projects are likely to be more expensive than AAUs as the former involve real costs. However, many demand-side governments have stated a preference for the project-based mechanisms over and above trading of AAUs as they generate real environmental benefits. This tendency will support Russian activities on JI as against direct sales of the country's surplus emissions.

A further change will be the need for the Russian government to establish the required compliance institutions in order to host JI projects. Without this legislation, which was not necessary for hosting pilot projects, transfers of generated credits could not be made and any proposed projects would be meaningless to investors (see Chapter 9). If Russia cannot fully comply with the administrative requirements of the Kyoto regime, Russian projects will be implemented as Track 2 JI projects. This procedure is slower and more bureaucratic than the Track 1 procedure and would add to transaction costs. However, it might provide Russia with additional opportunities to launch future projects prior to achieving full eligibility under the Kyoto Protocol. Chapter 9 discusses the compliance institutions further.

Table 8.4 summarizes the main challenges facing future project developments in Russia.

Conclusions

In addition to domestic compliance institutions, the Russian government must establish administrative responsibilities and procedures for JI in order to attract future projects. Currently, the lack of administrative support and of a responsible agency to write off ERUs by Letters of Approval is blocking otherwise competitive JI projects. Consequently, problems similar to those experienced in the AIJ phase prevail. However, the momentum generated by Russia's ratification of the Kyoto

Protocol in November 2004 has already spurred the government to reform the domestic institutional system (see Chapter 10). The recent approval of Russian project proposals by various European governments (see Chapter 7) – subject to Letters of Approval by the Russian government – is an encouraging sign that the implementation-level problems experienced during the pilot phase are being overcome. Together with the ongoing interest of Russian organizations to produce complicated project proposals for bidding tenders, this provides evidence that managerial capacity and the commitment to project implementation have both improved since the pilot phase.

The character of funding-related problems has changed as JI projects will produce credits carrying economic value, thereby creating incentives for the private sector to invest. However, competition in the market is growing, and Russia could find proposed JI projects ruled out on grounds of cost or preparedness.

9 RUSSIAN INSTITUTIONAL COMPLIANCE UNDER KYOTO

The compliance system under the Kyoto Protocol is both unique and one of the most comprehensive and rigorous regimes in multilateral environmental agreements. The compliance regime consists of a Compliance Committee which is made up of two branches: a Facilitative Branch and an Enforcement Branch. The Facilitative Branch provides advice and assistance to aid compliance; the Enforcement Branch determines whether Parties comply with their emission target and reporting requirements, and decides on the consequences for Parties that do not meet their commitments. There are sanctions for non-compliance, the most important of which is losing eligibility to participate in implementing the Kyoto mechanisms.[1]

Currently, Russian greenhouse gas inventories and reporting to the Secretariat of the UNFCCC do not comply with the Kyoto requirements. In the event of continued non-compliance, Russia would not be entitled to participate in the Kyoto mechanisms. This would mean that Russian credits and allowances could not be included in the Kyoto markets. Thus, Russian compliance is important not only to Russia but also to the whole Kyoto regime.

This chapter reviews the various requirements for compliance under the Kyoto Protocol and the current status of and prospects for Russian compliance. Contrary to what some observers have stated, it argues that compliance under Kyoto is possible and affordable for Russia.

Compliance requirements

Compliance under the Kyoto regime consists of two main elements: quantitative and institutional compliance. *Quantitative compliance* refers to meeting emission limitation or reduction commitments established for the industrialized countries (Annex 1 Parties) by the Kyoto Protocol.

Institutional compliance covers all the other elements of compliance required by the Protocol, i.e. establishing a national system of emissions monitoring and reporting.

It is unlikely that Russia will experience difficulties in achieving quantitative compliance, which tends to be the main concern in most Annex B countries. As discussed in Chapter 3, owing largely to the sharp reduction in Russia's total greenhouse gas emissions since the base year of 1990, Russian emissions are unlikely to exceed the target of 1990 levels before the end of the first commitment period in 2012.[2]

Consequently, institutional compliance is the main focus of the discussion on Russian domestic implementation. Russia has experienced problems with its institutional system established to implement the UNFCCC. Russian national reporting and greenhouse gas inventories are behind schedule and international expert review teams have criticized the quality of reporting. Moreover, as discussed in Chapter 8, the Russian pilot project registration and approval system for AIJ suffered from serious institutional problems.

Full Track 1 compliance allows an Annex 1 Party to participate in all the Kyoto mechanisms, and requires that the country:

- is a Party to the Kyoto Protocol;
- has calculated its Assigned Amount;
- has in place a national system of greenhouse gas inventories;
- has in place a national greenhouse gas registry;
- has submitted the most recent required inventory, a National Inventory Report and the Common Reporting Format; and
- has submitted supplementarity information.

All this has to be implemented according to the required guidelines and rules.

Track 2 compliance facilitates participation in Joint Implementation only under a UNFCCC supervisory committee, and requires that a country:

- is a Party to the Kyoto Protocol;
- has calculated its Assigned Amount; and
- has in place a national greenhouse gas registry.

Table 9.1: Full and Track 2 compliance requirements

	Full compliance	Track 2 compliance
Ratification	X	X
Calculation of AAUs	X	X
GHG inventory system	X	
GHG registry	X	X
Reporting	X	
Supplementarity information	X	
Verification of reduction by supervisory committee		X

Source: UNFCCC. FCCC/CP/2001/13/Add.2. Available at *http://cdm.unfccc. int/Reference/COPMOP/decisions_17_CP.7.pdf.*

Track 2 compliance would make the JI procedure much more bureaucratic and slow, which is not desirable from the investor country's point of view. Achieving full compliance should be a priority for Russia as only this will allow it to administer its JI projects without external interference and to participate in international emissions trading. Table 9.1 summarizes the differences between full and Track 2 compliance requirements.

Elements of institutional compliance

In order to become a Party to the Kyoto Protocol, a country has first to ratify the Protocol. This is a prerequisite for participation in the Kyoto mechanisms, which is likely to be the area of greatest interest to Russia. The recent Russian ratification establishes the basis for the need to achieve compliance under Kyoto. In order to achieve institutional compliance, a Party must have:

- implemented domestic policies and measures;
- constructed annual greenhouse gas inventories according to the Intergovernmental Panel on Climate Change (IPCC) Guidelines;
- established a registry to keep track of domestic emissions and implementation of the Kyoto mechanisms , comparing them with the commitments under Kyoto to ensure compliance; and

- reported all this to the UNFCCC Secretariat in the required schedule.

Of these, the inventory requirements are likely to be the most challenging and complicated issue for Russia in achieving compliance.

Greenhouse gas inventories in Russia

Inventories of greenhouse gas emissions and removals are the core of the national institutional system as they serve as a basis for measuring quantitative compliance as achieved through domestic policies and measures and the Kyoto mechanisms. Moreover, institutional compliance requirements for reporting and monitoring are based on greenhouse gas inventories.

Historically, Russian greenhouse gas inventories have been published in the National Communications, as required by the Convention. Russian inventories are available for the years 1990–99 but are currently running behind schedule. Inventories tend to lag by about two years; in mid-2005 the Russian reporting gap was about three years in addition to the standard lag.

A further problem with existing inventories is that the data are mainly from federal-level statistics, which are generally too aggregated to comply with the IPCC Guidelines. This said, the National Communications have improved over time and the Russian team has added more greenhouse gases over the years and clarified emission source categories. But no emitting factors[3] or uncertainty estimates have been provided. Thus far, the Russian administration has also failed to use the Common Reporting Format (aimed at standardizing reporting by Annex 1 Parties), or to submit National Inventory Reports which provide information on national approaches to the internationally agreed methodologies.

Some private companies have created their own greenhouse gas inventories. The electricity giant RAO UES Rossii is the best-known case and produces annual inventories.[4] Gazprom has also created an inventory but it has not yet been published. Other companies too have generated greenhouse gas inventories – for instance the Solombala and Arkhangelsk pulp and paper mills[5] and the aluminium giant RusAl. Other big companies have the relevant data available as required by the federal statistics office, but this is not public information.

Official responsibility for greenhouse gas inventories rests with the federal administration. However, some regional administrations have already produced local inventories (see Table 9.2). This is an important development; even though the federal level has responsibility for overall national climate policy, the detailed data required by the IPCC methodologies are not always available in official federal-level statistics, and data published by regional statistics offices can often fulfil these requirements.[6] Thus it should be possible to implement greenhouse gas inventories that are consistent with the IPCC Guidelines.

In 2001 the federal government upgraded the methodology of the national inventories by including activity data for different sectors of the national economy. Also a nationally adjusted version of IPCC software is now available. This should make it possible for Russia to produce inventories according to the 1996 Revised IPCC Guidelines and to comply with the UNFCCC Common Reporting Format. In addition, experts have carried out further studies of country-specific emission factors in the agriculture and forestry sectors.[7] Regional experiences demonstrate the feasibility of such practices and the resulting enhanced accuracy of source categories; the regional inventory of Arkhangelsk is based on the IPCC Guidelines.[8]

Quality and availability of Russian greenhouse gas inventory data

Estimating emissions from energy production and consumption data is fairly easy for Russia because the energy sector data are generally of good quality. This is extremely important since, as already indicated, the energy sector is the dominant emitter of greenhouse gases. However, data on energy use for transport, and municipal and residential fuel consumption, are of lower quality.[9] Moreover, there are either no data or only very approximate data available for gas flaring by oil producers or methane from coal-mining activities. These omissions may cause problems with greenhouse gas inventories.

Emissions from industrial processes are in general quite well monitored and available at the federal level, although it can be difficult to identify the types of industrial processes. A key problem is that data on the emissions of some of the most powerful greenhouse gases (HFCs, PFCs and SF_6)[10] are not available.[11]

The quality of regional forestry inventories varies and the forestry statistics data are not consistent with the IPCC requirements. This is partly

due to the lack of a clear division of responsibilities for data collection between the federal and regional levels.[12] Russia could fulfil the inventory requirements on land use change and forestry activities under Article 3.3, although additional land use sinks defined under Article 3.4 are more problematic. There are no federal statistics on the waste sector. The number of landfills is recorded at the regional level, but additional data collection activities and analysis will be needed to achieve compliance. The role of regional actors is crucial in this sector.[13]

The national statistics service does collect the relevant data on agriculture, but it is highly aggregated and very approximate as the structure of Russian agriculture changed dramatically with the collapse of the Soviet Union and transition from state to private ownership. Despite this, agricultural statistics are not a great problem for Russia as emissions from this sector amount to only about 4% of the total.[14]

Non-compliance related to greenhouse gas inventory failure

The UNFCCC has introduced rules which regulate how compliance of greenhouse gas inventories is evaluated. According to the UNFCCC Secretariat,[15] the following reporting failures can result in non-compliance:

- Complete annual inventory (both Common Reporting Format and National Inventory Report) is not submitted within six weeks of due date.
- A large key source that accounts for 7% or more of annual emissions is missing.
- Total adjustments in any year are greater than 7% of submitted inventory.
- Sum of the total adjustments for any years of the commitment period exceeds 20% of submitted emissions.
- A key source that accounts for 2% or more of emissions is adjusted in three consecutive years.

Even though there are obvious gaps in the Russian inventory, it should be possible to collect most of the missing data. Reporting inventories in the required schedule would eliminate the first potential failure. The second rule leaves headroom for a problem area smaller than 7% of the total annual emissions. If associated gas flaring counts here it

could potentially cause a problem, but for instance failure to report emissions from agriculture would fit within the limit of 7%. Russia is, however, at risk of non-compliance on the third point as the inaccuracy of the Russian inventory is likely to exceed the 7% cut-off. Reform of the data collection system could solve this and other potential problems concerning adjustments listed in the last two points.

Greenhouse gas inventories in Russian regions

Table 9.2 lists the Russian regions that had implemented or were planning to implement greenhouse gas inventories in 2002. If the listed regions finished and maintained their greenhouse gas inventories, these inventories would cover about one-eighth of the regions. The importance of current regional efforts is demonstrated by the fact that these regions account for more than 17% of both population and industrial volume (see Table 9.2). But as the table makes clear, only some of the

Table 9.2: Status and importance of Russian regional greenhouse gas inventories in 2002

Regions	Start of inventory	Years covered	Status of inventory activities	% of total Russian population living in region (2001)	% of total Russian industrial volume (2001)
Novgorod	1999	1990–2001	Ongoing	0.49	0.41
Sakhalin	2000	1990–1999	Finished	0.41	0.56
Chelyabinsk	2000	1990–1999	Finished	2.52	2.90
Khakassia	2000	1990–1999	Finished	0.40	0.25
Arkhangelsk	2000	1990–2002	Ongoing	0.99	0.74
Nizhny Novgorod	2001	1990–2001	Finished	2.50	2.14
Sverdlovsk	2001	1990–2001	Ongoing	3.16	3.57
Leningrad			Planned	1.15	1.26
Moscow			Planned	5.90	5.60
Total				17.52	17.43

Sources: Leneva (2002), pp. 21–2; Goskomstat (2002a), pp. 82–3; Goskomstat, (2002b), pp. 49–51.

regions are updating their inventories (ongoing activities), and quite a few of them finished their activities some years ago. Other regions, such as Saratov, Kemerovo, Karelia and Moscow oblast, are planning inventories.[16]

The prolonged uncertainty surrounding Russian ratification of the Kyoto Protocol may explain some of these delays in developing accurate inventories, as without ratification there were no guarantees that any projects would materialize. The fact that Arkhangelsk region took further steps towards implementation of the Kyoto Protocol within a couple of months of Russian ratification by establishing a regional commission focusing on the issue[17] provides evidence to support this theory. However, the role of regions in implementing Kyoto remains unclear. This may discourage early action, although the Ministry of Natural Resources has also initiated new inventories in some other regions.

Based on a major research and demonstration programme in 1999–2002, some Russian experts argue that regional experts are in a position to compile a full regional inventory. However, to do so would require a clear understanding of the IPCC Guidelines, and access to guidance on transforming the regional data into the IPCC format. In this regard, a federal-level 'hot line' could be of assistance.[18]

Other aspects of institutional compliance

Policies and measures in Russia

The Kyoto Protocol requires that Annex 1 Parties achieve their emission reduction or limitation commitments chiefly through domestic policies and measures. Russia has introduced some domestic policies and measures as a domestic greenhouse gas reduction strategy in the National Communications but has experienced problems in implementing them.[19] However, Russia (like other countries in transition) is in a peculiar position in that greenhouse gas emissions are likely to remain below the base-year level regardless of further domestic policies and measures, so these are not crucial to quantitative compliance during the first commitment period. In theory at least, domestic emission reduction activities remain important, as emission reductions achieved through the Kyoto mechanisms have to be supplemental to domestic actions in

Annex 1 countries,[20] but even so specific policies and measures can be largely regarded as a reporting formality from the Russian point of view.

Registry

While Russia has yet to establish a national registry – a national log that would register international transactions at the state level – this is not a serious problem. A simple registry could be created fairly easily as it need only operate at the federal level if there are no plans to establish a domestic national emissions trading system. There are now plans to establish such a registry (see Chapter 10).

National reporting

Current Russian national reporting practices could cause a compliance problem, but could be improved fairly easily. Drafting National Communications and reporting annual greenhouse gas inventories is the responsibility of Roshydromet together with the Institute of Global Climate and Ecology. National Communications submitted so far fulfil the requirements of the Convention but are insufficiently detailed to comply with the requirements of the Kyoto Protocol. This problem could be solved by greater coordination and a reallocation of responsibilities. In the past, Roshydromet has drafted the sectoral chapters of the National Communications and then collected comments from the relevant sectoral ministries. While it is clear that no single agency can cover all the ground required by national reporting, further involvement of the sectoral ministries at an early stage would contribute to the depth of the relevant chapters. Reporting itself is unlikely to be an issue as long as the quality of greenhouse gas inventories improves.

Summary of gaps and status of compliance

Table 9.3 summarizes the status of the elements of Russian compliance. This highlights the fact that while Russia is likely to achieve quantitative compliance, it is weak on policies and measures and behind on registry and reporting requirements. However, the major problem for Russia is the inadequate state of its inventories – the very basis of institutional compliance.

The federal-level data used so far are too aggregated and some additional data collection will be required as will greater regional involvement.

Table 9.3: Status of Russian compliance

Element of compliance	Current status in Russia	
Emissions	Russia well below target	+ +
Policies and measures	Enough to show activity	+
Registry	A simple registry could be quick and cheap to establish	−
Reporting	Easy to improve with better inventories and more cooperation between administrative units	−
Inventories	Data missing, quality not consistent with IPCC requirements	− −

Key: + + will not cause problems; + will not cause serious problems; − will cause problems but easy to solve; − − will cause problems, difficult to solve.
Source: Korppoo (2004).

The main gaps in inventory data are as follows:

- forestry inventories not consistent with IPCC requirements, quality varies between regions;
- data for gas flaring and coal-mine methane not available or very approximate;
- data for waste sector not available;
- data for agriculture very approximate;
- some problems with industrial activity data;
- lack of some data for transport, municipal and residential fuel consumption.

Inventory methodologies are also inconsistent with the IPCC Guidelines, although this problem could probably be solved at the same time as reform of data collection and by providing domestic experts with the necessary resources and training to apply this methodology.

Affordability of institutional compliance

Earlier sections have highlighted the scope for use of regional data and local expertise for the national inventory. While it would be inefficient

in resource terms to allocate the whole inventory to individual regions, costs could be kept low through rational application of regional expertise to data collection and analysis tasks that cannot be completed at the federal level.

Russian options for the creation of a registry include either developing its own, or buying or otherwise acquiring one from another country. Neither of these options is expensive in the case of a simple registry. Improving the quality of reporting could also be quite cheap and involve little more than some reallocation of existing resources, with more time allowed for sectoral agencies to draft the relevant chapters at the expense of a central agency, particularly given the difficulties faced by a single agency in covering all the expert areas.

The expertise needed to establish a domestic compliance system is available in Russia, and relying on domestic civil servants and experts could deliver affordable institutional compliance and ensure that this experience is available in future. Using external (especially foreign) consultants instead of Russian civil servants would cost more and would be unlikely to deliver a better compliance system.

Conclusions

This chapter demonstrates that while practices in Russia currently fall short of compliance requirements under the Kyoto Protocol, it is both possible and feasible for Russia to achieve full compliance, and this is in the country's interest. Achieving full compliance would, however, require some extra work and attention by the federal administration as, in the past, a lack of coordination and cooperation between agencies has undermined Russian inventories and reporting to the UNFCCC. These problems should be easy to solve if there is a real political will to do so.

The trickiest problems to resolve relate to missing data required for a greenhouse gas inventory, but even in this case it should be possible to collect adequate data with the involvement of regional actors. There are also many well-trained Russian experts who would be able to create an institutional system which delivers full compliance under Kyoto. Overall, the cost of Russian compliance seems proportionate to the benefits.

10 PROGRESS AND PROSPECTS FOR IMPLEMENTATION

Introduction

Russian participation in the Kyoto Protocol will involve complex and bureaucratic tasks to ensure institutional compliance with provisions under the treaty. At a fundamental level, the Russian government will need to decide which of the Kyoto mechanisms will be prioritized as this will determine the institutional requirements. The government approved a National Action Plan on Kyoto Protocol implementation in Russia (NAPR) at the end of February 2005 and this is now in the process of realization.

This chapter examines developments since ratification. Drawing on both published information and 'off the record' conversations with Russian officials and analysts, it provides a forward-looking assessment of progress in – and prospects for – implementation of the Protocol in Russia.

Institutional developments

Pre-ratification

While preparations for ratification began in 2002, practical progress on institutional development was modest prior to the actual decision to ratify in late 2004. As discussed in Chapter 9, not only did Russia fail to deliver the greenhouse gas inventories and reports required by the Convention but also all Kyoto-related activities virtually stalled. In part, this may have been due to the uncertainty associated with the prolonged ratification process. By July 2004 most Russian key agencies were sceptical about Russia joining the Kyoto Protocol. Other factors in the delay included infighting between departments, vested interests of individuals and changes in staff, combined with a lack of clear institutional responsibilities.[1]

Far-reaching administrative reforms in the Russian government in 2004 did not dramatically change Russian climate policy or its implementation. However, the Ministry of Industry and Science and the Ministry of Energy were merged to form the Ministry of Industry and Energy and a new agency, the Russian Committee of Technical Inspection (RosTechNadzor), relevant to Kyoto administration, was formed under the newly established ministry.

The government's decision to put the ratification decision before the Duma in September 2004 stimulated discussion on new institutional arrangements for implementing the Kyoto Protocol. Thus the development of a National Action Plan of Russia to facilitate implementation began even before official ratification.

National Action Plan

The NAPR is a comprehensive plan covering the legislative and institutional arrangements required for implementatiin of the Kyoto Protocol.[2] These include all requisites for institutional compliance, GHG inventory, registry and reporting requirements, sectoral tasks and responsibilities for future negotiations. A 'living document', it is intended to be – and is being – upgraded over time.

The Plan also outlines institutional arrangements identifying tasks, lead agencies and timelines for action. These are shown in Table 10.1. The division of responsibilities is clearly defined; the first agency on the list for each task can be regarded as the leading agency. The importance of the Ministry of Economic Development and Trade (MEDT) is recognized in its leadership of preparations for the Kyoto mechanisms. MEDT bears the main responsibility for reporting to domestic bodies. It also heads up a new Interagency Commission on the Kyoto Protocol established in June 2005 to facilitate cooperation between ministries. Roshydromet continues as the leading agency in GHG inventories, international reporting and international negotiations, and the preparation of the National Communications (although the Ministry of Natural Resources is likely to play a much more important role in this last task than previously). The Ministry of Natural Resources will develop the national registry. Sectoral tasks on forest sinks, agriculture and energy have been allocated to the specialized ministries and agencies.

The timelines established in the NAPR emphasize the creation of compliance institutions and a domestic system for implementing the

Table 10.1: National Action Plan of Russia: main tasks, schedule and responsible agencies

Task	Schedule	Responsible agencies
Kyoto mechanisms		
Preparation of legislation on implementing Kyoto mechanisms	Mid-2005	MEDT
Preparation of national JI administration	Mid-2005	MEDT
Negotiations on JI and IET with international financial organizations and foreign investors	N/A	MEDT, MIA
Preparation of guidelines for Russian companies implementing CDM projects	Late 2005	MEDT
GHG inventory and registry		
Preparation of legislation on establishment of GHG registry	Late 2005	MNR with MEDT
Establishing system for inventory of GHGs and sinks	Mid-2005	Roshydromet with MNR and other related agencies
Implementing inventories for 1990–2004 and submitting them to UNFCCC	Mid-2006 – and then annually	Roshydromet with MNR and other related agencies
National and internal reporting		
Preparation of National Communications to the UNFCCC	2006	Roshydromet with MEDT and other agencies
Effective cooperation of agencies: reporting back to government and Duma on implementation of Kyoto	Reporting annually from 2005	MEDT leading, sectoral agencies assist on reporting
Reporting back to the Duma on implementation of the Kyoto mechanisms	Annually	MEDT with other relevant agencies
Sectoral tasks		
Market reform: reduction or removal of market structures that do not support emission reductions	Various	Sectoral agencies: Minregion, Rosstroi, FAS, MIE
Energy sector: emissions, efficiency improvements etc.	Various	MIE
Forestry and agricultural sinks	Various	MNR with forestry organizations and Ministry of Agriculture
Research and development on emission reduction and CO_2 capture technologies	Various	MES, Rosnauka, sectoral agencies

Task	Schedule	Responsible agencies
International negotiations		
Representing Russia in UNFCCC COP/ MOPs	N/A	Roshydromet, MNR & MIE
Negotiating with other Parties on specific issues	N/A	Relevant government organization
Future commitments		
Preparation of Russian position on MIE	Late 2005	Roshydromet, MIA,
second commitment period		
Preparation of emission scenarios until 2020	End of 2007	MEDT

Key: Ministry of Economic Development and Trade (MEDT); Ministry of Industry and Energy (MIE); Ministry of Natural Resources (MNR); Ministry of Education and Science (MES); Ministry of International Affairs (MIA); Federal Agency for Science and Innovation (Rosnauka); Federal Anti-monopoly Service (FAS); Ministry of Regional Development (MinRegion); Federal Agency of Construction and Housing (Rosstroi).
Source: Plan of combined activities to implement the Kyoto Protocol and UNFCCC in Russia, draft.

Kyoto mechanisms. Most of these tasks are scheduled to be finished by the end of 2006. Timelines in the NAPR suggest that the government should have approved the rules and procedures for JI projects by summer 2005. However, in practice completing a full system for implementing the Kyoto Protocol in Russia could easily take a couple of years.

Whether or not these institutional arrangements will deliver remains to be seen. In important respects, responsibilities remain similar to before and certainly Roshydromet's past record on developing monitoring systems under the Convention is not encouraging. This said, the prospect of Russian participation in the Kyoto mechanisms combined with further involvement by MEDT may provide a sufficient stimulus for delivery.

Institutional challenges

A key challenge for many agencies could be funding. Implementation of the NAPR is expected to be financed from agency funds allocated prior to the ratification decision, and thus no earmarked funds are immediately available. This means that poorer agencies are likely to struggle to find the resources required to implement the Plan. Current government budgetary

arrangements may also hinder the development of GIS. In the first half of the decade, the government has directed almost all non-budgetary funds (except the pension and social insurance funds) to the federal budget, and federal-level ecological funds have ceased to exist; pollution fees collected by the government are directed to the public budget.

A second challenge relates to personnel dynamics within government departments. Kokorin[3] describes how, in the past, personal interests and staff changes have had a significant influence on advancing climate change policies in Russia. While motivated individuals can facilitate progress by creating a favourable basis for action at a higher level through anticipation of requirements, historically some officials have been reluctant to devote energy to tasks that do not involve new funding or profit. For instance, this has been the case with the UNFCCC reporting by Roshydromet. Thus, staff changes can influence the whole approach of an agency. A further ongoing problem is that few, if any, Russian officials are working on the Kyoto Protocol full-time. Thus, successful implementation of the treaty is likely to require greater staff stability, human resources and administrative discipline than have previously been experienced.

A third issue is corruption, which is endemic in many parts of the Russian bureaucracy. This both influences what is done and what is not and adds to transaction costs. Thus, some have proposed minimizing the involvement of officials in the distribution of revenues from activities under the Kyoto Protocol. Allocating revenues directly to enterprises implementing the projects is likely to prove efficient as they will have a vested interest in the success of the projects.

A final challenge is that many potential Russian hosts lack experience of preparing and implementing environmental investment projects. This was a problem in the pilot phase of AIJ (see Chapter 8) and since then only a couple of Russian actors have submitted competitive JI project proposals to bids. However, various business organizations and NGOs are providing support and expertise to companies and regions (see also Chapter 7). In particular, the National Carbon Sequestration Foundation (NCSF) has been working on capacity-building projects funded by the Global Environment Facility (GEF) and UNDP,[4] and RAO UES Energy Carbon Facility provides assistance to the local energy companies it owns.[5] In addition, WWF Russia, together with other organizations such as the Russian Regional Ecological Centre and the Centre for Energy Efficiency, has been spreading information by organizing and

supporting regional seminars. The Centre for Environmental Investments has prepared GHG inventories and project proposals for industrial actors.

Strategic options

Institutional requirements for implementation will depend on strategic decisions by Russia as to which of the Kyoto mechanisms to prioritize. As discussed in Chapter 9, some conditions have to be fulfilled in order to participate in the Kyoto mechanisms. First and foremost, Russia must comply with the institutional requirements of the Kyoto Protocol by establishing GHG inventory and registry systems and providing annual national reports. Beyond this, there is a second set of issues related to the practical readiness for implementation. Table 10.2 summarizes the main

Table 10.2: Strategic options and related requirements under the Kyoto mechanisms

Requirement implications	AAU trading			Domestic ETS + EU ETS	JI Track 1	JI Track 2
	Industry level	Unlinked govt-to-govt	GIS			
Focal point & procedures & strategic decisions	Yes	Yes	Yes	Yes	Yes	Yes
GHG inventory	Yes	Yes	Yes	Yes	Yes	No
GHG inventory according to UNFCCC rules	Yes	Yes	Yes	Yes	Yes	No
National allocation plan	Yes	No	No	Yes	No	No
International approval of transaction required	No	No	No	No	No	Yes
Project-based or linked emissions reductions only	No	No	Yes	Yes	Yes	Yes
Problems with additionality	No	No	No	No	No	Yes
Problems with transparency	No	No	Yes	Maybe	No	No
Problems with acceptance of units	Maybe	Maybe	No	Maybe	No	No

Source: Adapted from Mielke et al. (2004), p. 39.

institutional requirements and implications of various strategic options.

As highlighted in Chapter 9, the main difference between Track 1 and Track 2 JI options is that although the compliance rules are relaxed for Track 2 projects, such projects require international approval, whereas under Track 1 compliance rules are tighter but it is the project investor and host who determine the additionality bilaterally on the basis of general guidelines. Thus under Track 1 compliance Russia may apply more relaxed additionality rules under JI.

As discussed in Chapter 4, the domestic emissions trading scheme (ETS) refers to the option of a cap-and-trade system similar to the EU ETS, potentially providing access to the European market. But establishing such a system would require significant time and resources, and linking a domestic ETS to other schemes would require Track 1 compliance. A Green Investment Scheme (see Chapter 4) would fall into the category of AAU trading. However, this arrangement has some advantages compared to direct trading: greened trading could be linked to projects with criteria bilaterally agreed between countries and thus broader criteria or wider programmes than those under JI could be applied. GIS units would be more acceptable to the international community than direct trading with Russian surpluses owing to their higher environmental legitimacy. However, there might be problems over the transparency of recycling the revenue to be greened and a centrally managed fund might be susceptible to corruption.

AAU trading would require Track 1 compliance and might run into problems with acceptance of units by buyers. As discussed in Chapter 7, trading could occur either between private-sector actors (for which a national allocation plan would be required) or between governments. The EU has announced that companies are not allowed to use Russian AAUs in the EU market, and both Japan and Canada are officially against direct wealth transfers by buying Russian surplus AAUs without greening arrangements. However, this situation might change towards the end of the first commitment period should some countries be at risk of failing to meet their targets. Even so, some governments may prefer to overshoot their targets rather than — as some see it — undermining the environmental integrity of the Kyoto Protocol through 'hot air' trading.

Strategic priorities

Key criteria

Most Russian actors would like to see Russia as a market leader in the Kyoto market and to maximize revenues. But, a further key concern for Russian policy-makers is that the approach and projects selected should reflect wider social, economic and political objectives. Thus efforts are likely to focus on investments which not only reduce emissions but also meet wider objectives (such as energy efficiency, energy saving and forestry). This will require consideration not simply of near-term priorities, but also more strategically of what is required beyond 2012.

A number of criteria for strategic decisions over the use of the Kyoto mechanisms have been suggested, including:

- **Sustainable use of the new resource.** If project investments are backed with AAUs, then they should generate emission reduction not less than AAUs required to attract this investment.
- **Maximization of social and environmental benefits.** Projects should yield wide indirect benefits for Russia.
- **Credibility of the country.** National institutional systems and projects should conform with Kyoto compliance requirements.
- **Transparency and accountability.** Allowances should be awarded on a competitive basis with strict accountability for results.

Market considerations

There are uncertainties in both the Russian and the international carbon market, and 'rent-seeking' by some Russian and international traders adds to market volatility. Consequently, the Russian government seems likely to follow a conservative policy in the emerging carbon markets, at least initially – i.e. to avoid selling emission allowances at the current low prices paid for ERUs by bidding systems. Some Russian analysts believe that allowances are likely to be bought up at considerably higher prices closer to the end of the first commitment period in 2012.

MEDT regards the establishment of domestic ETS as a distant possibility given the level of engagement with industry that would be required. It has been argued that a traditional cap-and-trade scheme is unlikely to be considered because it does not appear to be politically viable. Big industry tends to be in favour of creating ETS;[6] however,

under current political conditions industry is kept at a distance from political decision-making.

Some have suggested establishing a pilot phase for the Kyoto mechanisms in Russia in order to test the institutional set-up and boost early projects prior to 2008. This could be based on voluntary participation by companies and involve government allocation of a share of the Russian national allowance which companies could then trade or use as JI project or loan guarantees. This would avoid the bureaucratic and risky process of state approval and substantially reduce transaction costs and investment risks, and thus attract investors. However, establishing a pilot phase prior to 2008 would be challenging as the Russian basic compliance institutions remain to be delivered.

Currently, JI bidding systems such as ERUPT, PCF or the Japan Carbon Fund (for further description see Chapter 7) are showing interest in JI projects at low prices (below €5–7/tonne of carbon dioxide) compared with the emerging EU ETS market price. This has been significantly higher during 2005, peaking at close to €30/tonne.[7] Some Russian observers regard this as a strategy to gain cheap allowances prior to the stabilization of the market price during the first commitment period. However, potentially Russia has the greatest share of the market, and this could allow the country to manipulate the price and volumes of supply in order to maximize revenues. It has also been argued that Russia could therefore apply a strategy to attract offers from investors and choose the most interesting of them which maximize benefits. Indeed, one option is for MEDT to put out a tender for project proposals based on bidding for the price of quotas. In such a scheme projects could be selected on the basis of the particular criteria outlined above. However, JI projects tend to be selected by investors' tender programmes, and it remains unclear how Russia could attract offers from investors.

The most attractive low-cost emission reduction projects are likely to be implemented first, and such options will become scarcer over time. Delay in the participation of private companies in project implementation will increase the risks of losing the potential for reducing low-cost emissions. This is because the investment cycle of energy-intensive industries tends to be long, and consequently projects cannot always be implemented at short notice. It would therefore be helpful to establish a legislative basis for the participation of businesses in Kyoto projects sooner rather than later.

Cooperation with American companies is another relevant factor, however; so far it is only a speculative issue, as discussed in Chapter 4. Despite the US administration's withdrawal from the Kyoto Protocol, there is a growing movement at the individual state level to limit greenhouse gas emissions. American companies might therefore buy emission permits from abroad, which could provide a new market for Russian allowances.

Role of regions and business

The role of the regions is scarcely reflected in the NAPR. This undermines the potential importance of their role in implementation of the Kyoto Protocol. Some regions will find it difficult to compete for projects with the well-prepared private-sector organizations such as RAO UES Energy Carbon Facility. However, there are regions which have expressed interest in hosting Kyoto projects. The best example is Arkhangelsk region which has already passed a regional decree to establish a Kyoto administration. In February 2005, this piece of legislation established a commission on climate change to coordinate limitation of emissions and JI project activities in the region.[8] The involvement of the regions could have long-term impacts on the division of the 'Kyoto cake' between Russian actors as benefits could potentially be divided more evenly around the country.

The role of industry in domestic implementation has not been further defined by the NAPR either, even though the document allocates the key decisions considering the involvement of industry to MEDT. Big business has been active in the preparations for Kyoto implementation and, as discussed in Chapter 7, is ready to implement projects as soon as the domestic administrative system is in place. Many industrial actors involved in the NCU would like to be allocated AAUs to manage.[9]

Future prospects

Features of future climate policy

Even though the implementation of the NAPR is still at an early stage at the time of writing, some key features of Russian climate policy seem clear.

- **An immediate focus on monitoring and reporting** as these are critical if Russia is to take advantage of the Kyoto mechanisms.

The NAPR addresses these issues but past experiences give rise to scepticism over the effectiveness and speed of implementation. Much will depend on individuals and the priority given to the task.

- **Near-term prospects are likely to focus on JI**, with a preference for projects and schemes that contribute to wider social and economic objectives. Track 1 compliance is still some way off, and the Track 2 option seems more possible initially. Russia is also well positioned to take advantage of JI tender programmes.

- **Russia is likely to hold on to surplus allowances** at least until the start of the first commitment period and possibly nearly until its end, in the hope of achieving higher carbon prices.

- **A Russian ETS is still some way off.** While some Russian analysts recognize that a domestic ETS would be an effective tool to limit emissions, and this might just be feasible by 2008, a strong political will would be required to deliver this.

- **Industry-level trading could minimize bureaucracy.** Industrial pressure groups are wary of the bureaucracy involved in project approval, and thus would rather manage AAUs themselves. However, on the basis of EU experience, it is difficult to see how this or even a pilot phase of allocations could be established prior to 2008.

- **The post-2012 negotiating position is likely to depend on both the effectiveness of Kyoto implementation – and thus gains – and wider national interests.** While successful implementation of the Kyoto mechanisms would undoubtedly incline Russia positively towards taking on future commitments, alignment with wider social, economic and political objectives will also be important. It remains to be seen whether the new administrative arrangement will deliver benefits from the Kyoto Protocol which could spur public opinion on to acceptance of further commitments.

Three scenarios

With the above in mind, there appear to be three broad paths which Russia may follow in its implementation of the Kyoto Protocol.

Fast track. The first and most optimistic scenario would be accelerated implementation and engagement in the Kyoto Protocol. In this case, the

Russian government follows the path of the NAPR and establishes domestic monitoring and reporting systems to meet UNFCCC requirements by 2007. Russia thus achieves Track 1 compliance from the beginning of the first commitment period in 2008, and all strategic options under the Kyoto mechanisms are open to it, including the possibility of creating a domestic ETS and linking with the EU ETS, and/or creating the GIS or other greening arrangements. Early JI projects could also be feasible. The certainty of Track 1 compliance leads to investors showing a keen interest in Russian allowances and projects. Encouraged by investment flows and associated reductions in emissions, together with wider social and economic benefits, Russia adopts a hard but progressive attitude to post-2012 commitments, seeking enhancement of the Kyoto mechanisms.

Slow track. Under the second scenario, progress on domestic implementation systems is modest, thus limiting the scope for use of the Kyoto mechanisms. Bureaucratic delays slow progress under the NAPR but domestic institutions are established and Track 2 compliance is achieved around 2008. However, it takes another couple of years for the system to be fully operational and Track 1 compliance is achieved only by the end of the first commitment period. The slow start reduces investor interest in Russian projects and only a few are being approved under governmental bidding systems. Thus benefits from JI are modest at best. In theory, full compliance allows Russia to trade in AAUs and Russia may gain from a last-minute rush from buyers as they seek to meet their own Kyoto commitments. However, the slow start means there is little time to establish greened trading systems, and bilateral agreements are likely to be required. It also makes the establishment of a domestic ETS and links with the EU ETS difficult or even impossible. With full compliance, but little immediate gain, Russia adopts a cautious approach to post-2012 negotiations with a focus on assured benefits and wider political gains, while the economic forecast may further influence these considerations.

Institutional paralysis. A third possible scenario is that the momentum gained from the ratification decision is lost and Russia makes only minimal progress on domestic monitoring and reporting systems. Russia does achieve Track 2 compliance during the first commitment period

but domestic legislation and bureaucratic constraints cause delays and projects are not competitive in governmental bids. Investor interest in projects is thus limited to those governments and companies with long-term and wider interests in Russia. Without Track 1 compliance, Russia is not entitled to participate in trading, and thus there is no basis for greening arrangements or access to the EU ETS market. Disillusioned over the benefits from the Kyoto Protocol and lacking of credibility in the international arena, Russia adopts an obstructive position in negotiations over future commitments, perhaps with constructive gestures only on technology and domestic initiatives.

A year after ratification

As of November 2005, the Russian government was, as anticipated, a little behind schedule in implementation of the NAPR overall, but significant developments took place during the summer and autumn of 2005.

On 1 July the Russian government established significantly stricter penalties on methane emissions that can be considered the first step towards limiting GHG emissions. A draft law on GHG emission regulations was being developed over the summer and autumn. Two different approaches have been under consideration: a radical approach aiming at reforming the whole system of environmental regulation, and a moderate approach focused on legally establishing JI activities as well as GIS. The second approach looked more likely at the time of writing.

The new Interagency Commission on the Kyoto Protocol first sat in July 2005. On the agenda was the realization of the NAPR, approaches to national legislation and agreements with other countries. A second meeting in November 2005 was tasked with approving JI procedures, national monitoring and inventory plans and final divisions of responsibilities between agencies – thus laying the critical groundwork for implementation of JI.

The Danish government contracted the first two JI projects with Russia in June 2005, and the Dutch ERUPT approved the first Russian project in September. The transfer of ERUs of the ERUPT project is subject to the Russian government signing a Letter of Approval for this project,[10] and the Danish government gave its Russian partners four months to obtain a Letter of Approval from the Russian government.[11] Although these were not delivered on time, it does seem that the Russian

government is moving towards finalizing the domestic JI system and that foreign investors are gaining some confidence in the process. It is also encouraging that a number of Project Idea Notes (PINs) and Project Design Documents (PDDs) have been developed for a range of project types.

A year after ratification, there was some evidence of enhanced international cooperation with the formation of a working group on the Kyoto Protocol under an ongoing EU–Russian Energy and Economic Dialogue.[12] In addition, a Japanese grant proposal on GIS and JI (via the World Bank) was under consideration as well as a (delayed) Danish and Global Opportunity Fund grant for 2003–05. Negotiations on bilateral agreements between Russia and other Annex 1 countries (including Denmark, France, Germany, Austria, Sweden and Canada) and coopera- tion in the Baltic Sea region were also progressing at various rates. Encouragingly, international support in the form of the EU's TACIS programme and the World Bank's Carbon Finance Technical Assistance Programme started in summer 2005 and spring 2005 respectively.[13]

Such domestic and international developments are promising for Russian participation in the Kyoto mechanisms but cannot be taken as a certain sign that Russia will follow the 'fast track' scenario described above. Indeed, the fact that Russia had yet to establish a domestic institutional system to achieve compliance suggests that the 'slow track' may be more likely.

Conclusions

At this stage, it is impossible to anticipate with any confidence which of the above paths Russia will follow. Not only could effective implemen- tation take several years but past experience shows that it cannot be taken for granted and there exists a real possibility of institutional paralysis prevailing. The scale of the task and internal barriers to be overcome means successful implementation will require sustained political will. The fact that President Putin has already enjoyed the international recognition of ratifying the pact may reduce the relevance of Kyoto, and the current positive developments could stop altogether. Russian observers are well aware that the country will comply with its 2008–12 emission limitation target even without measures to cut emissions (see Chapter 3). Consequently, institutional compliance is an issue only if

Russian decision-makers regard the Kyoto mechanisms as a desirable option. Indeed, the political benefits outweighed the economic opportunities in the ratification decision.

Russia is undergoing major political, administrative and economic reform. On his re-election in 2004, Putin gained more power that allows him to pursue further radical reforms, for instance replacing the election of regional governors with presidential appointments. Some of these changes – such as efforts to streamline the administration – may ease the implementation of compliance systems such as the Kyoto Protocol, while continued economic growth may help ensure that resources are available. Putin's involvement in the ratification decision may have created a personal commitment to the Kyoto Protocol, and thus he might oversee his administration's efforts to implement the pact.

After years of bureaucratic inertia on the Kyoto Protocol, the rapid agreement on a comprehensive plan for implementation is encouraging and suggests at least some such commitment to getting the Protocol up and running in Russia. Moreover, the emerging markets for credits could also provide a positive incentive to move quicker than in the past. Thus sufficient progress could well be made to enable significant Russian participation in the Kyoto mechanisms. However, this may require further personal leadership by the President, supported by the continuous engagement of other key players with Russia.

Nevertheless, if the Russian Constitution remains unchanged, the 2008 election will introduce a new president who might have a different approach to Kyoto. This might well change the approach to implementation at the beginning of the first commitment period.

11 CONCLUSION

This book paints a complex picture of Russia and the Kyoto Protocol, a picture that implies continuing uncertainty about the future 'terms of engagement'. The relationship of Russia to climate change and the Kyoto Protocol is one full of potential, but also many pitfalls. This enables the detailing of possibilities and themes, rather than predictions, of the country's future engagement with international efforts to tackle climate change.

The history of ratification outlined in Chapter 2 should be proof enough of this basic observation. It was a complex tale that baffled many international observers, who initially assumed that the Kyoto Protocol – which had secured the support of Russian negotiators through the difficult negotiations of 1997–2001 and appeared to be clearly in Russia's national economic interests – would be ratified as a matter of course. But although many in the West assume that Russians view such issues in terms of economics and international responsibilities, these seem to be minor considerations in a far more complex set of political debates within Russia. Issues relating to security, status, and national and geopolitical positioning, as well as the personal dynamics at play in the government and its administration, seem more important.

The potential

The evidence set out in Chapter 3 demonstrates that the Kyoto Protocol first-period commitments do not in any plausible way conflict with Russia's economic ambitions, but rather represent a potential resource in terms of surplus emission allowances and investment. The expectations of some prominent sceptics that Russian emissions would rise sharply with economic recovery are inconsistent with the experience of the transition process in other economies, and with international comparisons

of energy intensity; moreover, their predictions of rapid growth in Russian emissions have not been borne out by the most recent data. The evidence is also clear that reining in carbon dioxide emissions is consistent with wider political and economic objectives to upgrade the energy sector, improve energy efficiency and thereby reduce domestic costs and release more energy (especially gas) resources for export.

As Chapter 4 shows, Russia's engagement in the Kyoto mechanisms and emerging markets in emissions allowances and credits has considerable potential. For Russia, a key issue is the financial revenues that might accrue from the sale of its surplus emission allowances. However, while the potential revenue from such sales is considerable (as demonstrated in Chapter 5), it is still very modest in the context of the overall scale of the Russian energy sector and, indeed, the foreign revenue earned from oil and gas exports. The finding in Chapter 6 that the potential gains from increased exports of gas and some energy-intensive commodities may be comparable with the possible losses from reduced oil exports does not change this positive view of the overall economics of Kyoto, but helps to set it in the context of Russia as a major exporter of energy and energy-intensive products. From a purely economic standpoint, Kyoto will continue to be carefully scrutinized in terms of its impacts not just on finance but on the overall strategic positioning of these industries.

Harnessing this potential will therefore hinge upon engaging these interests constructively, in terms of both projects and relationships. As shown in Chapter 7, a wide range of potential energy-sector JI projects is available in Russia, with domestic actors willing and able to put them into practice. Energy efficiency and fuel-switching projects are among the most promising projects, but there is also scope for gas pipeline refurbishment and renewable energy. There is clear international interest in such possibilities, and tender programmes opened by governments and other investors provide a channel for cooperation. However, at the time of writing the lack of a clear division of responsibilities and domestic institutional support within Russia is holding back potential cooperation.

Unquestionably, Russia's decision to make energy a central theme of its G8 Presidency in 2006 – a commitment made in the context of the July 2005 G8 Communiqué on Climate Change – enhances the potential further. It offers the prospect of accelerating developments, and increasing also the attention devoted to energy efficiency and climate change considerations in the context of Russian energy and economic

developments. In the past, climate change cooperation between Russia and the key investor countries has suffered from a mismatch of expectations and lacked a platform for discussions; the G8 processes might help to overcome this.

The pitfalls

While there is great potential in Russia's engagement with the Kyoto Protocol, the scope for pitfalls seems equally great. The long history of 'Activities Implemented Jointly' (Chapter 8) makes for depressing reading and highlights the institutional incoherence of Russian policy towards climate change. Even when agreements have been struck with one party, and when there appear to be potential benefits all round, other players or a lack of clear administrative procedure and/or high-level commitment may block progress. Getting the institutional machinery to resolve differences and to approve projects has proved a consistent bottleneck.

Of course, this applies not just to climate-related projects, but across much of the experience of foreign investment in Russia. Most companies that have invested in Russia since the early 1990s, as the country has gradually opened up its economy, have found the road hard and long. Some have given up after experiencing long frustrations with bureaucracy, institutional paralysis and legal ambiguities; some have lost billions of dollars after changes to terms and conditions deprived them of expected benefits. Those that have benefited – or at least, gained enough confidence to expand operations into multi-billion-dollar investments – have done so on the back of a long process of building experience and relationships.

The biggest opportunities may arise if climate-related institutions and processes can somehow smooth the path of wider foreign investment (including that utilizing more advanced and efficient technologies); but there is as yet precious little sign of this. Coming from another direction, wider political, economic and administrative reform processes may help to streamline decision-making and reduce corruption, thus improving the prospects for implementation more generally. This is a slow process. To some degree, corruption and the ineffectiveness of policy implementation and rule of law may have been 'locked in' to the system owing to the benefits derived by a range of individuals from these shortcomings. Although in theory power is strongly centralized, these factors limit its

practical impact; President Putin can introduce changes on paper, but it is almost impossible to change everyday practices at the same pace.

These larger-scale problems of governance are reflected in the arena of climate change policy. The international negotiations have seen an uneasy compromise, at best, between the perceived interests of Roshydromet and those of the energy and economy-related ministries. The post-ratification process affirms the role of Roshydromet in the international negotiations, leaving it unclear how well the Russian positions will be integrated with domestic implementation possibilities and interests.

Also in the international arena, one other feature with which the international process will have to grapple is the level of suspicion directed at such processes. The underlying Russian psychology – reflected more generally in ambiguity towards foreign investment – appears very sceptical about the prospects for 'win-win' solutions. Yet as every business management student is taught, the prospects for successful negotiations depend heavily upon recognizing areas where all parties can gain. Assuming negotiations to be a competitive struggle in a zero-sum game is a poor basis upon which to build cooperative solutions.

The potential for continuing confusion and paralysis remains, not least because the Russian system hinges so much on the President, and it appears that climate and the Kyoto Protocol are not important issues to Putin in their own right. If Russia is not to miss the boat on opportunities under the Kyoto Protocol, there remains a need for clear high-level leadership and commitment. At this stage, it remains unclear whether this will be sustained post-ratification.

The possibilities

Nevertheless, focusing solely on the pitfalls risks painting a picture that is too negative. The ratification decision itself removed a major uncertainty, led directly to some clarification of responsibilities and kick-started a process of institutional reform. The NAPR allocated the Kyoto mechanisms to the Ministry of Economic Development and Trade, which at the time of writing is in the process of establishing a domestic system including a 'designated national authority' to authorize the crediting of JI investments and procedures.

At the minimum, Track 2 compliance under the Kyoto Protocol, and allocation of responsibility to transfer generated emission reduction units

to investors, will be required in order to facilitate JI cooperation. To support such efforts, the EU's approval of a major TACIS project to help Russia develop its capacity to implement the Kyoto Protocol is also a useful step forward. In all, the evaluation of Chapter 10 suggests that full institutional compliance is possible by the start of the first commitment period.

Many other possibilities emerge from ongoing developments. Not least, the EBRD Carbon Fund could play a major role, particularly if it is expanded to include the European Investment Bank. It could help to enhance the profile and status within Russia of the carbon agenda and the emergent carbon market. Such funds could also pave the way for development of functioning GIS-type transactions, utilizing larger parts of the Russian allowance surplus in ways that are seen to be mutually acceptable, and more efficient and effective than the project-based mechanisms alone.

More widely, the Russian decision declared in the G8 communiqué – that its G8 Presidency will include a focus on energy – makes Russia now centrally engaged in relevant international processes. Similarly, if Russia succeeds in its ambitions to join the WTO – now likely in 2007 – then the general investment climate in Russia could well improve, with positive implications for JI projects.

The G8 decisions, in particular, open up important possibilities, both through the specific elements of the Gleneagles Plan of Action and through the broader G8 Dialogue on Climate Change. It is too early to say much about the direction these may take as the G8 agreements were reached only shortly before this book was completed. But the broad-ranging agenda combined with the commitment to keep talking, including the energy focus of Russia's G8 Presidency and beyond, usefully complement the formal international negotiations on climate change. Prospects are further enhanced by the fact that Germany – Russia's single most important partner in energy trade – will take up the G8 Presidency after Russia. Moreover, the Dialogue on Climate Change is due to culminate the year after under the Japanese G8 Presidency, which offers important opportunities to take the climate/Kyoto agenda still further forward.

Looking forward

Although specific predictions are very hard, for the reasons set out in detail throughout this book, it does seem possible to offer some higher-level thoughts and identify themes on the overall direction of Russian involvement in the international climate change system.

First, for Russians, energy issues will take precedence over climate change issues. The preceding chapters have emphasized how central energy is to the Russian economy and to its international relationships. Climate change is not, and sufficient debate continues in Russia as to the pros and cons of a warming climate to make it difficult to gather strong political momentum behind the climate change agenda unless it is supportive of key elements in Russia's economic and political ambitions. In principle this is not difficult, since energy efficiency and natural gas offer positive contributions on both agendas; but harnessing such potential alignment will require political finesse.

Second, political considerations will continue to dominate economic ones, though the balance may gradually shift if and as Russia becomes more integrated in international markets and more open to foreign investment. However, it is not easy to predict exactly *how* these political considerations will play out. Russia now has strong stakes in both its European and its US relationships, which are likely to pull in opposite directions; and its Asian relationships, increasingly with China as well as with Japan and the central Asian countries, will also grow in importance. Despite the uncertainties, the weight accorded to countries supportive of the Kyoto process is likely to continue to grow. Barring a major political shock, such as a fundamental reversal in the direction of Russian evolution towards international engagement, Russia is thus extremely unlikely to back away from the Kyoto Protocol itself.

Third, despite this, institutional developments and clarifications will remain painfully slow and there continues to be some scepticism over whether or not Russia will get its act together. However, a spur is likely to be the reality of emerging markets and a growing realization that other transition countries – including Ukraine – could grab a larger share of the Kyoto prize, including GIS-type developments, if Russian involvement develops too slowly.

Fourth, and despite these nascent competitive pressures, the pace at which Russia deepens its engagement with the Kyoto Protocol and the

associated mechanisms may be very dependent upon the political sensitivity with which other countries approach it. Again the ratification experience is telling. At one stage, EU pressures and public remonstrations were almost certainly counterproductive. Lobbying in private, based on an understanding of Russia's real interests and sensitivities, is likely to be much more effective.

Fifth, and most soberingly, the disparity of expectations is likely to continue. Russia ratified the Kyoto Protocol partly on the expectation of financial gains through the Kyoto mechanisms. Suspicious of the market mechanisms – and also bruised by the US withdrawal – Russia sought formal guarantees, whereas the potential buying countries insisted that Russia had to accept the market-based nature of the mechanisms, while still highlighting Russia's apparently commanding position with regard to the availability of emission allowances. Russia expects the benefits to flow. Other countries are still waiting for Russia to provide greater institutional and legal clarity about the terms of trading through the mechanisms and greater assurances about the environmental legitimacy of such trades, and to play a generally more positive role in addressing the problems of climate change.

Thus the mismatch of mindsets continues, and remains the greatest challenge in engaging with Russia on climate change. The aim of this book has been to contribute to lessening that divide, and to building the mutual trust and understanding that has to underpin effective implementation and constructive future developments.

APPENDIX 1:
RUSSIAN PILOT PHASE PROJECTS

Table A.1: Russian AIJ projects approved by the UNFCCC

Project description	Project type	Investor country	Emission reduction (tCO$_2$e over project lifetime)	Project status
Horticulture project in Tyumen	Energy efficiency	The Netherlands	N/A	Completed
Modelling and optimization of grid operation of the gas transportation system 'Ushgorod Corridor' of Wolgotransgas	Energy	Germany	225,000	Completed
Reforestation in Vologda	Reforestation	USA	858,000	Cancelled
District heating in Tikhvin	Fuel switching	The Netherlands	N/A	Cancelled
RUSAGAS: Fugitive gas capture project, Pallasovka and Saratov	Fugitive gas capture	USA	30,955,750	Delayed
Sanitary landfilling with energy recovery in the Moscow region	Fugitive gas capture	The Netherlands	255,268	Completed

Source: Korppoo (2002b).

Table A.2: Russian unregistered pilot phase projects

Project description	Project type	Investor country	Emission reduction (tCO$_2$e)	State of implementation
Polessk ZKX	Fuel switching	Sweden	2,472	Completed
Polessk Regional Hospital	Energy efficiency, energy saving	Sweden	5,781	Completed
Infection hospital	Energy efficiency	Sweden	1,760	Completed
Pravdinsk district heating	Fuel switching, energy saving	Sweden	283,125	Completed
Specialist hospital	Energy efficiency, energy saving	Sweden	6,735	Completed
Driada Wood Processing Company	Fuel switching	Sweden	14,050	Completed
Children's Hospital No. 1	Energy efficiency	Sweden	14,344	Completed
Krasnyi Bor district heating	Fuel switching, district heating	Sweden	106,924	Completed
Lisino Forest College	Fuel switching, energy efficiency	Sweden	52,118	Completed
Pysochny fuel switching	Fuel switching	Sweden	30,052	Completed
Ilynsky Lesozavod boiler conversion	Fuel switching	Sweden	58,215 (projected)	Design and planning
Derevyanka & Derevyannoe fuel switching	Fuel switching	Sweden	20,225	Completed
District Heating Renovation in Lytkarino	Energy efficiency	USA	485,670 (projected)	Delayed
Cheliabinsk district heating	Energy efficiency	USA	N/A	Delayed
CO$_2$ reduction in Nizhny Novgorod region	N/A	The Netherlands	N/A	Completed

Project description	Project type	Investor country	Emission reduction (tCO$_2$e)	State of implementation
Energy saving in Tatar industry	Energy saving	The Netherlands	N/A	Cancelled
Nizhny Novgorod JI II	Energy saving	The Netherlands	N/A	Cancelled
JI in Gatchina	N/A	The Netherlands	N/A	N/A
Steamer boiler house in Nizhpharm	N/A	The Netherlands	N/A	Completed
Energy-efficient street lighting	Energy efficiency	The Netherlands	N/A	Completed
Clean air to city centre	N/A	The Netherlands	N/A	N/A
Karelia	N/A	Finland	N/A	Delayed
Pravdinsk, Kaliningrad	Renewable energy	Finland	N/A	Delayed

APPENDIX 2:
CARBON AND CO$_2$ READY RECKONER

The text refers to volumes of both carbon and carbon dioxide. These can be readily converted into each other using the following carbon conversion factors:

- 44/12 - when converting volume of carbon into a volume of carbon dioxide; and
- 12/44 - when converting volume of carbon dioxide into a volume of carbon.

Volumes (Mt)		Volumes (Mt)	
Carbon	**Carbon dioxide**	**Carbon dioxide**	**Carbon**
1	3.67	1	0.27
10	36.67	10	2.72
50	183.33	50	13.64
100	366.67	100	27.27

Prices (US$/tonne)		Prices (US$/tonne)	
Carbon	**Carbon dioxide**	**Carbon dioxide**	**Carbon**
1	0.27	1	3.67
3	0.82	3	11.00
5	1.36	5	18.33
10	2.73	10	36.67

NOTES

Preface

1 Radio broadcast, 1 October 1939, in *Into Battle* (1941).

Introduction

1 The 'Umbrella Group' consisted of almost all the industrialized countries outside the scope of the 'enlarged EU', the principal members being the US, Canada, Russia, Ukraine, Australia, Japan and Norway. Switzerland, New Zealand and Iceland later joined with South Korea and Mexico to form the 'Environmental Integrity Group'. See Chapter 2, and for a fuller account, Yamin and Depledge (2005) and Grubb et al. (1999).

2 Data for 1999 – the date of the latest inventory. Most methane and CO_2 emissions come from fuel consumption within the energy sector (including electricity and heat generation), but a significant quantity of CO_2 emissions arise from outside that sector as fuel is used for the production of mechanical energy. NC3 (2002). pp. 10–11.

3 RES (2003).

4 IEA (2004a).

5 RES (2003).

6 Ibid.

7 Bush (2003).

8 See OECD, *www.oecd.org/dataoecd/13/62/35032229.pdf*; and Central Bank of Russia, *www.cbr.ru/eng/analytics/macro/*.

2 The Road to Ratification and Beyond

1 As of 16 September 2005, 156 states and regional economic organizations (the EU) had ratified the Kyoto Protocol. In total, Parties account for 61.6% of Annex 1 emissions. Source: *www.unfccc.int*.

2 The US accounts for 25% of Annex 1 emissions, while Russia accounts for 17%.

3 Many of the discussions and interviews on which this work draws were conducted on a non-attributable basis.

4 Kotov and Nikitina (1997), pp. 349, 357.

5 Nikitina (2001).

6 Müller (1997).

7 Paradoxically, although action under the Kyoto Protocol may reduce oil demand, it is likely to increase demand for Russian gas (see Chapter 6). Russia has implicitly recognized this and has since joined with Canada in calling for credits for exports of 'clean' or 'cleaner' energy (read gas or nuclear in the case of Russia) in more recent international climate negotiations.

8 Moe and Tangen (2000), pp. 13–14.

9 OECD members outside the EU: Japan, the US, Switzerland, Canada, Australia, Norway and New Zealand, although Norway and, in particular, Switzerland, frequently stood apart from JUSSCANNZ positions. See Grubb et al. (1999), p. xxxi.

10 The Umbrella Group emerged at Kyoto and afterwards and brings the JUSSCANNZ countries (except Switzerland) together with Russia and Ukraine. See Introduction, note 1.

11 Moe and Tangen (2000), pp. 15–17.

12 A. Bedritsky and A. Metalnikov, 'Nekotorye voprosy peregovonov po ramochonoy konventsii OON ob izmenenii klimata: Ot Kioto do Buenos-Ayresa. *Energeticheskaya Politika*, no. 6, p. 23, 1998. Cited in Moe and Tangen (2000), p. 27.

13 Moe and Tangen (2000), pp. 15–17.

14 'Russia: wild card in Kyoto pact', *Wired*, 8 February 2003. Available at *http:www.climateark.org/articles/reader.asp?linkid=19997*.

15 Korppoo et al. (2001), p. 4.

16 Korppoo (2002a).

17 Korppoo (2003b).

18 'China, Russia back greenhouse gas pact', Reuters, 3 September 2002.

19 'Russia set to ratify Kyoto this year despite legal loopholes', Agence France-Presse (AFP), 24 September 2002.

20 'Kyoto Protocol awaits nod from Russia's Putin', *Planet Ark*, 7 July 2003, available at *http:/www.planetark.com/dailynewsstory.cfn/newsid/2141416/story.htm*.

21 NCSF and WWF Russia (2003).

22 'Russia's flip flop stance on Kyoto', Reuters AlertNet, 21 May 2005. Available at *http:www.alertnet.org/thenews/newsdesk/L04660261.htm*.

23 NCSF and WWF Russia (2003).

24 *Planet Ark*, 7 July 2003.

25 NCU (2003).

26 Moe and Tangen (2000), p. 26.

27 CAN Europe (2003). That said, levels of support vary across Russia. A WWF survey in November 2003 showed that in the provinces support for ratification was strongest in Volga, Ural and the Northwest, with only partial support in Siberia and Central provinces and minor support or low awareness in the South and Far East. WWF Russia (2003).

28 Kotov (2004a).

29 'Putin clear – studying national interest', *CTV*, 30 September 2003. NCSF and WWF (2003).

30 Kotov (2004a), p. 160.

31 'Russian opposition to Kyoto growing', *CNSNews.com*, 19 April 2004.

32 'Economy ministry urges Putin to ratify Kyoto Protocol', *Mosnews.com*, 15 April 2004, available at *http://www.mosnews.com/money/2004/04/15/kyotoprotocol.shtml*.

33 This does not necessarily reflect views across the whole RAS. In 2003, 250 members of the Russian Academy of Sciences signed an NGO petition in favour of ratification. However, influence remains with key individuals such as Izrael.

34 Kokorin (2003a).

35 Lo (2003), p. 38.

36 Illarionov's views have been widely reported. See for example 'Kyoto treaty discriminates against Russia', *The Russia Journal*, 6 October 2003, available at *http://www.russiajournal.com/news/cnews-article.shtml?nd =40734*; 'Russia's call on global warming', *ENN Affiliate News*, 10 March 2004, available at *http://www.enn.com/direct/display-release.asp?objid=D1D1366D000000FB353D59C;* 'Kremlin aide likens Kyoto Protocol to Auschwitz', Reuters, 14 April 2004; 'Kyoto an economic "death camp", flawed', *Petroleum News*, 7 March 2004, available at *http://www.petroleumnews.com/pnnew/688445152.html*.

37 Kotov (2004a), p. 160.

38 Kotov (2004a and 2004b).

39 Kotov (2004a), p. 160.

40 Ibid., p. 161.

41 Kokorin (2003b).

42 AFP, 26 September 2003.

43 'Russia: wild card in Kyoto pact', *Wired*, 8 February 2003 (see note 14).

44 *US-Russian Joint Statement on Climate Change Policy Dialogue*, US Department of State, 17 January 2003, available at *http://usinfo.state.gov/topical/global/climate/03012101.htm*; 'Russia set to ratify Kyoto Protocol – or will they?', 24 January 2004, available at *http://www.climateark.org/articles/reader.asp?linkid=19690*.

45 In a marked parallel with its apparent strategy to undermine the International Criminal Court, the US has been seeking bilateral agreements on climate change with as many countries as possible, seemingly in an attempt to subvert the Kyoto Protocol. Indeed, some have already suggested that a similar US–India bilateral agreement influenced proceedings at the eighth Conference of Parties in Delhi in 2002. Ott (2003).

46 Putin's willingness to work bilaterally even on international issues is illustrated by his efforts with President Bush to advance non-proliferation of nuclear weapons. Similarly, Russia's approach to international agreements such as the WTO has focused more on gaining concessions in exchange for its assistance than on cooperation and likemindedness as an end in itself. Lo (2003), p.120.

47 Translation of *ANSA Newswire*, 19 July 2003.

48 See for example the following: 'Russia urged to rescue the Kyoto pact', *The Guardian*, 26 February 2003, available at *http://www.guardian.co.uk/print/0,3858,4613439-103681,00.html*; 'Ministry says Russia is unlikely to ratify Kyoto Protocol in 2003', *The Russia Journal*, 9 September 2003; 'The EU appeals to Russia to ratify the Kyoto Protocol', *Climate Ark*, 14 March 2003, available at *http://www.climatearck.org/articles/reader?asplinkid=20985*.

49 'Russia 'undecided' on climate deal', BBC News, 29 September 2003. Available at *http://newsvote.bbc.co.uk*.

50 'Foreign minister denies dependence of Kyoto Protocol on Russia's decision', RBC, 23 January 2004.

51 Putin is reported to have said that Russia will not ratify without guarantees of income: 'Kyoto Treaty in the balance', BBC News, 29 September 2003. Available at *http://newsvote.bbc.co.uk/mpapps/pappstools/print/news.bbc.co.uk/1/hi/world/314918*.

52 Margot Wallström, 'Kyoto's noble cause', *The Moscow Times*, 9 October 2003.

53 'Russia nears crucial Kyoto decision', *Energy Argus*, October 2003.

54 Kokorin (2003 a), p. 4.

55 'Dark skies to the east', *The Economist*, 22 February 2004. European Commission (2004).

56 'France urges Russia to ratify Kyoto Protocol', Reuters, 29 September 2003.

57 'No link between Russia-EU relations and signing of Kyoto Protocol', *Eubusiness.com*, 4 February 2004.

58 'Enforcement of the Kyoto Protocol: will Russia ratify?', Centre for European Policy Studies (CEPS), 6 October 2003. Speakers, Alexander Roo, MEP and Jurgen Salay, EC. Available at: *http://www.ceps.be/wp.php?article_id=154*.

59 The EU-15 accounts for one-third of Russia's total trade, a figure which was estimated to increase to 50–60% with the EU's enlargement in 2004. Lo (2003), p. 60.

60 Lo (2003), p. 58.

61 'EU links Russia's WTO entry to Kyoto', Reuters, 28 January 2004. Available at *http://www.reuters.co.uk*.

62 Grubb and Korppoo (2004), pp. 18–19; Stern (2005).

63 Kotov (2004a), p. 158.

64 'EU offers backing for Russia WTO entry, gets Kyoto pledge', AFP, 21 May 2004. Available at *http://servihoo.com/channels/kinews/v3news_details.php?id=42648&CategoryID=47*.

65 'Putin to inform Schroeder and Chirac on Kyoto Protocol discussion'. *Carbono Brasil*, 1 September 2004. Available at *http://www.carbonobrasil.com/noticias.asp?iNoticia =5053&iTipo=12&page=16&idioma=2*.

66 Baker & McKenzie, 'Russia moves closer to Kyoto ratification', *Global Clean Energy and Climate Change Newsletter*, 28 October 2004.

67 Some external analysts have speculated that the timing could have been intended to deflect EU criticism over Chechnya, its handling of the Beslan hostage crisis and Putin's tightening grip on the regions, but this view is apparently not shared

in Russia. Putin is, however, adept at neutralizing effective criticism by juxtaposing good news with bad. See, for example, J. Mundy, 'Russia's Kyoto U-turn leaves Bush isolated in emissions row', *Guardian Weekly*, 8–14 October 2004.

68 Kotov (2004a), p. 164.

69 'Commentary: Monument to the pendulum – why did Russia vacillate on Kyoto?', Bellona, 20 October 2004. Available at *http://www.bellona.no/en/energy/35649.html*.

70 'Moscow's stance on Kyoto "smart"', *The Washington Times*, 18 October 2004.

71 'Russia may ratify Kyoto Protocol in 2004 – Zhukov', Interfax, 7 October 2004.

72 RES (2003).

73 'Russian–US Arctic climate monitoring station to open in north port of Tiksi', Itar Tass, 31 March 2005.

74 US Department of State, *Joint Statement of the United States and the Russian Federation following the Third Meeting of the US-Russia Climate Change Policy Dialogue Working Group*, 31 May 2005. Available at *http://www.state.gov/g/oes/rls/or/48445.htm*.

75 See, for example, 'Russian advisor discusses climate change issues', Australian Broadcasting Corporation, 18 February 2005. Available at *http://www.abs.net.au/lateline/content/2005/sl1307945.htm*. 'Q&A: Putin's Critical Adviser, Time's Yuri Zarakhovich talks with Andreì Illarionov, the Russian Presidents's key economic adviser who resigned this week'. Available at *http://www.time.com/time/world/printout/0,8816,1145192,00.html* (31 December 2005).

76 See, for example, 'Climate change: not a global threat', *RIA Novosti*, 20 August 2005, available at *http://en.rian.ru/analysis/20050623/40748412.html*; and 'Kyoto Protocol to destroy Russian economy with unnecessary payments', *Pravda*, 7 May 2005.

77 *The* Science and Environment Policy Project, 2 July 2005. Available at *http://www.sepp.org/weekwas/2005%202.htm*.

78 A recent warning of the effect of ongoing global warming on Siberian peat bogs was sounded by Russian and American scientists in August 2005. Russian has warmed by some 30C in the last 30 years and the permafrost is already melting. This followed earlier findings from western Siberia that thousands of lakes in eastern Siberia have disappeared in the last 30 years. See F. Pearce, 'Climate warming as Siberia melts', *New Scientist*, 11 August 2005, p. 12.

79 See Alaska Regional Assessment Group, *The Potential Consequences of Climate Variability and Change* (Fairbanks, AK: Center for Global Change and Arctic Systems Research, University of Alaska, 1999); H. Cole et al., 'The economic impact and consequences of global climate change on Alaska's infrastructure', in G. Weller and P. Anderson (eds), *Assessing the Consequences of Climate Change for Alaska and the Bering Sea Region. Proceedings of a Workshop on the Consequences of Global Change for Alaska and Bering Sea Region, 29–30 October 1998* (Fairbanks, AK: University of Alaska, 1999).

80 According to Article 27 of the Kyoto Protocol, to withdraw from the Protocol

any Party must give written notification to the Depositary. Any such withdrawal then takes effect a year after receipt of this notification.

3 Russian Energy and Carbon Dioxide Emission Prospects

1 NC3 (2002) gives overall greenhouse gases in 1999 at 61.5% of 1990 levels, and CO_2 emissions at 63.5%. Taking account of the managed forest allowance, a rough estimate is that energy-related CO_2 emissions could increase by about 60% from these levels and still be compatible with Russia's Kyoto limit (1990 levels x $0.62 \ x \ (1+0.6) = 1999$ levels).

2 International estimates of these parameters for 1990 and 1991 differ markedly, in part because of limited data availability during a period of economic and political upheaval. For this reason, many studies use 1992 as a start point. Accurate and agreed emissions data for 1990 are of particular importance as this is the base year for commitments under the Kyoto Protocol.

3 RES (2003).

4 The energy intensity of the economy is the total energy consumption per unit of GDP. The carbon intensity is the carbon emissions (or equivalent in GHG) per unit of energy consumption.

5 IEA (2004a).

6 World Bank (2003).

7 OECD (2004).

8 Mitchell (2002).

9 'Will Russia double GDP without high oil prices?', *Analiticheskii Bankovskii Zhurnal*, No. 8, August 2003. Available at: *www.worldbank.org.ru*.

10 Bashmakov (2004).

11 RES (2003).

12 Russian Ministry of Energy. Figures for 2000 measured in PPP 1995 US$.

13 IEA (2004a).

14 The Strategy's own price projections show no incentive to switch from gas to coal until at least 2006. Beyond this, reductions in gas subsidies could favour coal – a complete removal of gas subsidies is projected to result in fuel prices 36% higher than those for coal. However, the greater efficiency, low capital cost, environmental advantages and ease of transportation of gas relative to coal seem likely to dictate against large-scale switching.

15 NC3 (2002). The underlying economic and energy assumptions used in these projections are slightly different from the most recent Energy Strategy and, in particular, represent a more limited range of GDP growth rates than is possible.

16 IEA (2004a).

17 CEPA (2004).

18 The model is based on the relationship: $C = GDP \ x \ E \ / \ GDP \ x \ C \ / \ E$. In this equation: C represents GHG emissions (in units of carbon equivalence), E is total

energy consumption and GDP is Gross Domestic Product.

19 Illarionov (2004).

20 'Russia examines its carbon future', *Carbon Market News*, 8 August 2005, available at *www.pointcarbon.com*.

4 Russian Opportunities in the Kyoto Market

1 Tangen et al. (2002), p. 19.

2 Mielke et al. (2004).

3 Fankhauser and Lavric (2003).

4 For further information see Tangen et al. (2002), and Korppoo (2003a).

5 The Prototype Carbon Fund maintains that the relevant paragraph in the Marrakech Guidelines for the Implementation of Article 6 'is not entirely clear. When it provides that "ERUs shall only be issued for a crediting period starting after the year 2008" it is not clear if this means the ERUs can only be generated by such projects after 2008 or whether the ERUs generated between 2000 and 2008 are "held in suspension" until 2008. If it means the latter then this could mean that PCF projects generating ERUs prior to 2008 could "bank' those early ERUs until the crediting period begins.' PrototypeCarbon Fund, *Policy Framework for Obtaining Early Credit for Emission Reductions in JI Projects. Updated Version in the Light of the Marrakech Accords*, PCF Implementation Note Number 8, January 2002, *http://prototypecarbonfund.org/router.cfm?Page= Operations*.

6 'Russian reality test for Kyoto', *The Japan Times*, 12 December 2003, available at *www. japantimes.co.jp/cgi-bin/geted.pl5?ed20031212a1.htm:* 'Mr. Illarionov … said … that the protocol was inequitable since it did not include major developing nations such as China and India.'

7 Decision 21/CP.8, Annex B. Available at *www.unfccc.int*.

8 *http://prototypecarbonfund.org/router.cfm?Page=Operations*.

9 Ibid.

10 Tangen et al. (2002), p. 65.

11 European Commission (2003a).

12 European Commission (2003b).

13 For an overview of funds, see 'Following the money', in *Global Carbon 2005*. A special Carbonexpo supplement to *Environment and Carbon Finance*, May 2005. Environment Finance, London, pp. S28–S33.

14 Lecocq and Capoor (2005).

15 Nord (2004).

16 'Canada – Dion promotes emissions trading scheme', *Canadian Press*, 12 August 2005. Available at *http://www.ctv.ca/servlet/ArticleNews/story/CTVNews/ 1123797240194_119206440/?hub=Canada*.

17 Rector (2004).

18 Lecocq and Capoor (2005).

19 The Climate Stewardship Act of 2003, sponsored by Senators McCain (R) and Lieberman (D), would cap US greenhouse gas emissions and establish a national greenhouse gas trading system. The bill was narrowly rejected by the Senate in October 2003 by 43 votes to 55. Efforts to introduce the bill in a revised form in the Climate Stewardship and Innovation Act in June 2005 failed by a wider margin of 38 votes to 60. However, in June 2005, the Senate adopted by 53 votes to 44 a non-binding *Sense of Senate Resolution*, sponsored by Senator Bingaman (D) and supported by Senator Domenci (R). This both affirmed the science of climate change and called for a 'national program of mandatory market-based limits and incentives on greenhouse gases'. See AAEA (American Agricultural Economics Association) (2005), *Climate Change. Votes on McCain/Lieberman Global Warming Bill and Senate Resolution*, available at *http://www.aaenvironment/ ClimateChange.htm*; and 'Climate change Senate resolution backs mandatory emission limits', *Science* 309 (2005), p. 32, available at *http://www.sciencemag.org*.

20 Mielke et al. (2004).

21 Ibid.

22 Lecocq and Capoor (2005).

23 'Russian companies want to accelerate Kyoto implementation', *RIA Novesti,* 25 September 2005.

5 The Value to Russia of Emissions Trading

1 European Environment Agency (2004).

2 Grubb (2003).

3 Karas (2004).

4 Grubb (2003.

5 Grubb (2003).

6 Dutch Minister of Economic Affairs, quoted in *Point Carbon,* 21 November, 2003. Available at *www.pointcarbon.com*.

7 UK Presidency of the EU 2005, *EU Investment in the Kyoto Mechanisms*. Available at *http://europa.eu.int/comm/environment/climat/pdf/eu_mechanisms_kyoto.pdf*.

8 Moe and Tangen (2000).

9 Springer (2003) classifies the models used into a number of categories: 'integrated assessment models', which examine physical and social process; general equilibrium models, 'top-down' models that capture the impact of energy policy on other sectors; emission trading models, such as the CERT model analysed in greater detail below; neo-Keynesian macroeconomic models, another form of top-down model; and energy system models, 'bottom-up' models which have a detailed representation of the energy sector.

10 Full details of the study, the model used and the results can be found in CEPA (2004).

11 All four growth scenarios result in an upper limit equilibrium price of US$5.9 per

carbon tonne when a 100% export cap is applied. However, this result is not shown in the range of prices as this high price is not actually associated with Russia's maximizing its benefit. Under a 100% cap, emissions trading does not result in any overall reduction global emission; thus despite a complete restriction on emissions surplus trading there is still a demand, supply and therefore price for carbon abatement (CEPA, 2004).

12 CEPA (2004).

6 Indirect Effects of Emissions Trading

1 For example, Holtsmark (2003).

2 A detailed analysis of the impact in the power sector is given in Reinaud (2003).

3 Hagem et al. (2004).

4 IEA (2004a).

5 Ibid. Shell's Vice President for Russian, Caspian Region and Southeast Europe, Martin Bakman, actually expected that Russian exports of gas to Europe would double over the next 20 years. Quoted on *www.Pravda.ru*, 29 October 2003. Nevertheless there remains significant debate around EU demand for Russian gas.

6 'Globalization and Energy' is a joint project between STATOIL and the Foundation for Research in Economics and Business Administration (SNF). The purpose is to present key features of importance for the long-term development in the world economy, and to enable the user to retrieve information that can help in assessing the future situation in vital markets. Further details available at *http://www.snf.no/statoil/global/*.

7 *Times Online*, 22 October 2003.

8 See, for example, Holtsmark (2003) and Hagem et al. (2004).

9 IEA (2004a).

10 By the summer of 2005, some impacts of current high oil prices on consuming countries were already becoming apparent. See, for example, 'South East Asia and oil: The black and blue stuff', *The Economist*, 13–19 August 2005, p. 47.

11 The embodied carbon content of a product relates to the amount of CO_2e produced per unit of production through the burning of fossils fuels.

12 Russian State Customs Committee, 2004. Available at *www.customs.ru*.

13 Dudek et al. (2004).

14 World Aluminium, 2004. Available at *www.world-aluminium.org*.

15 EIA (2005)

16 See, for example, 'The black and blue stuff', *The Economist* (note 10 above); 'Fuel costs drive switch to superminis', *The Times*, 1 September 2005, p. 50; 'EU pushes biofuel to fight climate change, high oil', Reuters, 11 September 2005, available at *http://wwww.alertnet.org/thenews/newsdesk/L1195109.htm*; J. Waggoner, 'Crazy oil prices fuel alternative opportunities', *USA Today*, 2005, available at *http://usatoday.com/money/perfi/columist/waggon/2005-08018-fuel-x.htm*.

7 Joint Implementation in Russia: Prospects and Value

1 Zelinsky (2004).

2 Projects of the Energy Carbon Fund, 26 July 2005. Available at *http:// www.carbonfund.ru/en/show.cgi?projects/27projects.htm.*

3 Social Forum on Climate Change, *Working Group 4 Draft Report,* 2003. Available at *http://www.environmentaldefense.org/documents/2935_WG4Final_FirstDraft_EN. pdf.*

4 G. Walters, 'Kyoto financial rewards: who will benefit?', *St Petersburg Times,* 15 June 2004. Available at *http://www.sptimes.ru/archive/times/977/news/b_12716.htm.*

5 Mielke et al. (2004), p. 28.

6 Vasiliev and Safonov (2003).

7 Korppoo and Ikeda (forthcoming 2006).

8 'Toyota Tsusho seeks Russian carbon credits', *PointCarbon* 24 February 2004. Available at *http://www.pointcarbon.com/article.php?articleID=3292,* accessed 1 September 2005.

9 Foreign Affairs Canada, Canada's Clean Development Mechanism and Joint Implementation Office: Program Description and Assistance Criteria. Available at *http://www.dfait-maeci.gc.ca/cdm-ji/program_desc-en.asp,* accessed 1 September 2005.

10 Karas (2004).

11 Deutsche Energie Agentur website: Eastern Europe and Russia, 10 August 2005. Available at *http://www.deutsche-energie-agentur.de/page/index.php?id=717&L=4.*

12 Mielke et al. (2004), p. 20.

13 IEA (2004b), p. 86.

14 Mielke et al. (2004), p. 21.

15 Gazprom (2002).

16 IEA (2004a).

17 RES (2003).

18 Pluzhnikov (2003).

19 RES (2003).

20 Berdin et al. (2003).

8 Lessons Learnt from AIJ Pilot Projects

1 FCCC/CP/1995/7/Add.1. Decision 5/CP.1 Activities Implemented Jointly under the pilot phase. Available at *http://unfccc.int/resource/docs/cop1/ 07a01.pdf#page=18.*

2 'On the preparation of the ratification of the Kyoto Protocol to the UN Framework Convention on Climate Change' [*O podgotovke k ratifikatsii Kiotskovo Protokola k ramotsnoj konventsii OON ob izmenenii klimata*], Russian Government Press Release No. 580, 11 April 2002.

3 Moe and Tangen (2000), pp. 14–16.

4 Kokorin (2000), p. 7.

5 It was difficult to track down all the similar projects because they were not registered

under AIJ; however, the main investor countries reported some 25 projects.

6 Data no longer available on the Roshydromet website.

7 This study is based on six registered and 23 unregistered pilot projects. Only two of the projects were related to activities outside the energy sector. The data reported in this chapter are based on questionnaires and interviews with seven governmental and private-sector investors from the Netherlands, Germany, Finland, the United States and Sweden. All had been involved in pilot projects implemented in Russia. In addition, some of the informants provided project-specific documents, and three Russian experts involved in the projects reported their experiences.

8 Korppoo et al. (2001), p. 4.

9 Kokorin (2000), p. 7.

10 Dudek and Wiener (1996), p. 20.

11 See, for example, IEA (2002), p. 23.

12 Fankhauser and Lavric (2003), p. 17.

9 Russian Institutional Compliance under Kyoto

1 UNFCCC website, Compliance under the Kyoto Protocol: COP7 and the Marrakesh Accords, 25 July 2005. Available at *http://unfccc.int/kyoto_mechanisms/compliance/items/3024.php*.

2 RES (2003).

3 According to well-informed sources, apparently emitting factors are available but were not presented for internal political reasons. A key issue is one of commercial confidentiality: including such factors requires revealing data to potential future competitors.

4 Zelinsky (2003).

5 Environmental Investment Center (2002), p. 8.

6 Leneva (2002), p. 21.

7 Ibid., pp. 20–21.

8 Environmental Investment Center (2002), p. 25.

9 Leneva (2002), p. 38.

10 Over a 100-year period, HFCs are between 150 and 11,700 times more powerful as greenhouse gases than CO_2, while PFCs are between 6,500 and 9,200 times more powerful and SF_6 is 23,900 times more powerful.

11 Leneva (2002), pp. 26 and 38.

12 Arkhipov and Lyubimov (2003, pp. 22–3.

13 Unpublished interview with Alexey Kokorin, WWF Russia. January 2004.

14 NC3 (2002).

15 UNFCCC Secretariat (2004).

16 Leneva (2002), pp. 21–2.

17 'Arkhangelsk rabotaet po protokolu', *Bizniz-klas,* 31 January 2005. In Russian. Available at *http://www.arhpress.ru/bizklass/2005/1/31/6.shtml*.

18 Gritsevich et al. (2001), p. 7.
19 UNFCCC (2000).
20 Kyoto Protocol, Articles 6.1, 12.3 and 17.

10 Progress and Prospects for Implementation

1 Karas (2004) and Kokorin (2003a).
2 Berdin (2005) and Pluzhnikov (2005).
3 Kokorin (2003a and 2004).
4 Available at *http://www.nopppu.ru/en/,* 25 July 2005.
5 Available at *http://www.carbonfund.ru/en/show.cgi?about.htm,* 25 July 2005.
6 *The NCU Concept of the Emission Reductions Trading System,* National Carbon Union, 2005. Available at *http://www.natcarbon.ru/en/analytical/system/.*
7 'Europe greenhouse gas trade hots up as prices soar', Reuters, 13 July 2005. Available at *http://www.planetark.com/dailynewsstory.cfm/newsid/31644/story.htm.*
8 Arkhangelsk oblast administration, *On the Climate Change Commission and Control of Greenhouse Gas Emissions,* Decree by Head of Administration, 25 February 2005.
9 *The NCU Concept of the Emission Reductions Trading System* (see note 6).
10 *SenterNovem,* 30 September 2005. First ERUPT 5 contract signed in Russia. Available at *http://www.senternovem.nl/carboncredits/news/first_erupt_5_contract_ signed_ in_russia.asp.*
11 'First JI agreements with Russia', *DanishCarbon.dk,* 28 June 2005. Available at *http://www.mst.dk/transportuk/01070100.htm.*
12 EC (2005).
13 Berdin (2005).

REFERENCES

Arkhipov, V. and A. Lyubimov (2003). 'Forest Inventory Reform in Russia', in A. Niskanen, G. Filioushkina and K. Saramäki (eds), *Economic Accessibility of Forestry Resources in North-West Russia*, EFI Proceedings No. 48, European Forest Institute, Joensuu, Finland.

Barker, T., L. Srivastava et al. (2001). 'Sector Costs and Ancillary Benefits of Mitigation', in *IPCC Third Assessment Report: Climate Change Mitigation* (Cambridge: Cambridge University Press), Chapter 9.

Bartsch, U. and B. Müller (2000). 'Impacts of the Kyoto protocol on fossil fuels', in L. Bernstein and J. Pan (eds), *Sectoral and Economic Costs and Benefits of GHG Mitigation. Proceedings of an IPCC Expert Meeting, 14–15 February 2000* (Bilthoven, Netherlands: Technical Support Unit, IPCC Working Group III), pp. 37–53.

Bashmakov, I. (2004). *Russian GDP Doubling, District Heating and Climate Change Mitigation*. Presentation to 'UNFCCC Workshop: Climate Change Mitigation: Vulnerability and Risk, Sustainable Development, Opportunities and Solutions', 19 June, Bonn.

Berdin, V. (2005). *Implementation of the Kyoto protocol in Russia*. Available at *http://www.iea.org/Textbase/work/2005/5ghg/6_berdin.pdf*.

Berdin, V., S. Vasiliev, V. Danilov-Danilyan, A. Kokorin and S. Kuraev (2003). *Kyoto Protocol: Politics, Economics, the Environment*, WWF booklet. Available at *http://www.wwf.ru/pic/docdb//publ/kyoto_QA_eng.pdf*.

Berg, E., S. Kverndokk and K. E. Rosendahl (1997). 'Market power, international CO_2 taxation and oil wealth', *Energy Journal* 18, pp. 33–71.

Bernard, A., S. Paltsev, J. Reilly, M. Vielle and L. Viguier (2003). *Russia's Role in the Kyoto Protocol*, MIT Joint Program on the Science and Policy of Global Change.

Bush, K. (2003). *Russian Economic Survey – September 2003*. (Washington, DC: Center for Strategic and International Studies).

CAN Europe (2003). *Ratification Calendar*. Available at *http://www.climnet.org/EUenergy/ratification/calendar.htm*.

CEPA (2004). J. Mirrlees-Black, N. Novčić, M. Grubb, A. Korppoo and D. Newbery, *Costs and Benefits to the Russian Federation of the Kyoto Protocol*.

Report to the Department for Environment, Food and Rural Affairs, UK (London: Cambridge Economic Policy Associates).

Donovan, D., K. Schneider, G.A. Tessema and B.S. Fisher (1997). *International Climate Change Policy: Impacts on Developing Countries*. ABARE Research Report 97–8 (Canberra: Australian Bureau of Agricultural & Resource Economics).

Dornau, R. (ed.) *Greenhouse Gas Market 2004: Ready for Take Off* (Geneva: International Emissions Trading Association).

Dudek, D. and J. Wiener (1996). *Joint Implementation, Transaction Costs and Climate Change* (Paris: OECD).

Dudek, D., A. Golub and E. Strukova (2004). *Economics of the Kyoto Protocol for Russia: The Mystery of Russian Ratification* (Washington, DC: Environmental Defense).

EIA (2005). *World Oil Market and Oil Price Chronologies: 1970–2004*. Available at: *http://www.eia.doe.gov/emeu/cabs/chron.html*, March.

Environmental Investment Center (2002). *Energy Sector Development and Climate Change Mitigation in Arkhangelsk Oblast* (Arkhangelsk: Greenhouse Gas Inventory and Registry Bureau, Environmental Investment Center).

European Commission (2003a). *Directive 2003/.../EC of the European Parliament and of the Council establishing a scheme for greenhouse gas emission allowance trading within the Community and amending Council Directive 96/61/EC.* Commission of the European Communities, Brussels. (Provisional unofficial version incorporating final amendments adopted by the European Parliament at its second reading on 2 July 2003 and accepted by the Council at its meeting of 22 July 2003.)

European Commission (2003b). *Proposal for a Directive of the European Parliament and of the Council amending the Directive establishing a scheme for greenhouse gas emission allowance trading within the Community, in respect of the Kyoto Protocol's project mechanisms.* COM(2003) 403 final. Commission of the European Communities, Brussels, 23 July.

European Commission (2004). *Communication from the Commission to the Council and the European Parliament on Relations with Russia.* COM(2004) 106, 9 February 2004.

European Commission (2005). *EU–Russia Relatiions.* Available at *http://europa.eu.int/comm/external_relations/russia/intro/*.

European Environment Agency (EEA) (2004). *Greenhouse Gas Emission Trends and Projections in Europe in 2004. EEA Report No 5/2004* (Luxembourg: Office for Official Publications of the European Communities).

Fankhauser, S. and L. Lavric (2003). 'The investment climate for climate investment: Joint Implementation in transition countries', *Climate Policy* 3, pp. 417–34. (Also published as EBRD Working Paper No. 77.)

Fenman, G. (ed.) *International Politics of Climate Change: Key Issues and Critical Actors* (Oslo: Scandinavian University Press).

Gazprom (2002). *Report on Environmental Protection 2002.* Available at *http://www.Gazprom.ru/eng/articles/article8939.shtml.*

Ghanem, S., R. Lounnas, D. Ghasemzadeh and G. Brennand (1998). 'Oil and energy outlook to 2020: implications of the Kyoto Protocol', *OPEC Review* 22, pp. 31–58.

Goskomstat (2002a). *Rossiiskii Statisticheskii Jezhegodnik 2002*, Moscow.

Goskomstat (2002b). *Promishlennost Rossii 2002*, Moscow.

Gritsevich, I., A. Kolesov and A. Kokorin (2001). 'Multi-regional project to develop monitoring and reporting capacity for multiple greenhouse gases in Russia', *Energy Efficiency,* 34, January–March.

Grubb, M. with C. Vrolijk and D. Brack (1999). *The Kyoto Protocol. A Guide and Assessment* (London: Royal Institute of International Affairs/Earthscan).

Grubb, M. (2003). 'The economics of the Kyoto Protocol', *World Economics* 4(3), pp. 143–89.

Grubb, M. (2004). *Russian Energy and CO_2 Emissions and its Kyoto Target: Prospects and Determinants.* Briefing Note, Sustainable Development Programme (London: Royal Institute of International Affairs).

Grubb, M. and A. Korppoo (2004). 'Beyond ratification', *Environment Finance*, November, pp. 18–19.

Hagem, C., S. Kallbekken, O. Mæstad and H. Westskog (2004). *Market Power with Interdependent Demand. Sale of Emission Permits and Natural Gas from the Former Soviet Union,* CICERO Working Paper 2004:01, Oslo.

Holtsmark, B. (2003). 'Russian behaviour in the market for permits under the Kyoto Protocol', *Climate Policy*, 3.

IEA (2002). *Russia Energy Survey* (Paris: IEA/OECD).

IEA (2004a). *World Energy Outlook 2004* (Paris: OECD/IEA).

IEA (2004b). *Renewables in Russia: From Opportunity to Reality* (Paris: OECD/IEA).

Illarionov, A. (2004). 'The Kyoto Protocol and Russia: what is to be done?'. Presentation at the National Press Club, Washington DC, 30 January 2004.

Karas, J. (2004). *Russia and the Kyoto Protocol: Political Challenges.* Briefing Note, Sustainable Development Programme (London: Royal Institute of International Affairs).

Kokorin, A. (2000). *Review on Joint Implementation and Emission Trading in the Russian Federation,* Background Paper (Moscow: WWF Russian Programme Office).

Kokorin, A. (2003a). 'What the Kyoto Protocol means for Russians', *Change* 64, pp. 1–5.

Kokorin, A. (2003b). 'Russia's [non]ratification of Kyoto – economic plan or political chaos?', *Hotspot*, Issue 30, November (Brussels: CAN Europe).

Kokorin, A. (2004). *Who is Who in Problem of Climate Change in Russia* (Moscow: Institute of Ecological Consulting).

Korppoo, A. (2002a). 'Russian ratification process: why is the rest of the world waiting?', *Climate Policy* 2, pp. 387–93.

Korppoo, A. (2002b). 'Barriers to Joint Implementation in Russia: Lessons learnt from the Activities Implemented Jointly pilot phase'. Master's thesis, Department of Regional Studies and Environmental Policy, University of Tampere, Finland.

Korppoo, A. (2003a). *Implementing Kyoto in Russia and CIS: Moving from Theory to Practice,* Climate Strategies Workshop Report. Available at *http://www.climate-strategies.org/russiaworkshop.htm*.

Korppoo, A. (2003b). 'Forging alliance with Russia: the example of the Green Investment Scheme'. *Climate Policy* 3, pp. 67–76.

Korppoo, A. (2004*). Russia and Compliance under Kyoto: An Institutional Approach*. Briefing Note, Sustainable Development Programme (London: Royal Institute of International Affairs).

Korppoo, A. (2005). 'Russian energy efficiency projects: lessons learnt from the Activities Implemented Jointly pilot phase', *Energy Policy*, Vol. 33, No. 1, January, pp. 113–26.

Korppoo, A. and Ikeda, K. (forthcoming, 2006). 'Russia and Japan: combining energy and climate goals'. Accepted for publication in the *International Review for Environmental Strategies*.

Korppoo, A., C. Vrolijk and J. Stern (2001). *Energy and Climate: Russian-European Partnership*. Workshop Report, Energy and Environment Programme (London: Royal Institute of International Affairs).

Kotov, V. (2004a). 'The EU–Russia ratification deal: the risks and advantages of an informal agreement', *International Review for Environmental Strategies*, 5 (1), pp. 157–65.

Kotov, V. (2004b). *Greening of Policies: perspectives in Russia.* Available at *http://www.fu-berlin.de/ffu/akumwelt/bc2004/download/kotov_f.pdf*.

Kotov, V. and E. Nikitina (1997). 'To Reduce or Produce? Problems of Implantation of the Climate Change Convention in Russia', in J.B. Poole and R. Guthrie (eds), *Verification 1996: Arms Control, Peacekeeping and the Environment* (Boulder, CO: Westview Press), pp. 349, 357.

Lecocq, F. and K. Capoor (2005). *State and Trends of the Carbon Market 2005* (Washington, DC: World Bank and International Emissions Trading Association).

Leneva, M. (2002). *Possible Approaches and Next Steps for the Development of a National Inventory System in the Russian Federation* (Moscow: Centre for Environmental Economic Research and Information). Available at *http://www.oecd.org/dataoecd/5/37/2467501.pdf*.

Lindholt, L. (1999) *Beyond Kyoto: CO$_2$ Permit Prices and the Markets for Fossil Fuels*. Discussion Paper No. 258, August (Oslo: Research Department of Statistics Norway).

Lo, B. (2003). *Vladimir Putin and the Evolution of Russian Foreign Policy* (Oxford: Royal Institute of International Affairs/Blackwell).

McKibbin, W., M. Ross, R. Shackleton and P. Wilcoxen (1999). 'Emissions trading, capital flows and the Kyoto Protocol', *Energy Journal*, Special Issue, 'The Costs of the Kyoto Protocol: A Multi-model Evaluation', pp. 287–334.

Mielke, E., P. Spedding, N. Morton, V. Ahuja, R. Beaver and M. Backman (2004). *Russia and Kyoto: Match Made in Heaven?,* Dresdner Kleinwort Wasserstein Research.

Mitchell, J. (2002). *Renewing Energy Security*. Briefing Paper, Sustainable Development Programme (London: Royal Institute of International Affairs).

Moe, A. and K. Tangen (2000). *The Kyoto Mechanisms and Russian Climate Politics* (London: Royal Institute of International Affairs).

Müller, B. (2004). *The Kyoto Protocol: Russian Opportunities,* Briefing Note, Sustainable Development Programme (London: Royal Institute of International Affairs), March.

Müller, F. (1997). 'Russia and Climate Change', in G. Fenman (ed.), *International Politics of Climate Change: Key Issues and Critical Actors* (Oslo: Scandinavian University Press).

NC3 (2002). *Third National Communication of the Russian Federation,* The Interagency Commission of the Russian Federation on Climate Change, Moscow. Available at *www.unfccc.int*.

NCSF and WWF Russia (2003). National Carbon Sequestration Foundation and WWF Russia, 'Kyoto Protocol in Russia: slow, difficult, but forward!', 9 December. From *bounce-climate-l-135287ists.iisd.ca* on behalf of *sokolov @ruscarbon.com*.

NCU (2003). 'Non-profit partnership', presentation to side event at UNFCCC COP9, 8 December.

Nikitina, E. (2001). 'Review article: Russia: climate policy formation and implementation during the 1990s', *Climate Policy* 1, pp. 289–308.

Nikitina, E. (2003). 'Russia and Kyoto: is it make or break?', presentation, Ecopolicy Research and Consulting and Institute of World Economy, Russian Academy of Sciences.

Nord, L. (2004). 'Norway and the EU Emissions Trading Scheme. Establish a Link Under Article 25 or Join the EU ETS by Implementing the Directive?', in R. Dornau (ed.), *Greenhouse Gas Market 2004: Ready for Take Off* (Geneva: International Emissions Trading Association), pp. 96–8.

OECD (2004). *OECD Economic Survey of the Russian Federation 2004: The Sources of Russian Economic Growth* (Paris: OECD).

Ott, H. (2003). 'Warning Signs from Delhi. Troubled Waters Ahead for Global Climate Policy', published under the title 'Global Climate' in *Yearbook of International Environmental Law,* Vol. 13 (2002) (Oxford: Oxford University Press).

Pershing, J. (2000). 'Fossil Fuel Implications of Climate Change Mitigation Responses', in L. Bernstein and J. Pan (eds), *Sectoral Economic Costs of GHG Mitigation,* Proceedings of an IPCC Expert Meeting, IPCC Working Group III (Bilthoven, Netherlands: National Institute of Public Health and the Environment).

Pluzhnikov, O. (2002). 'Russia - View on Kyoto Protocol from today's perspective and tomorrow's', presentation to Climate Change Conference, Royal Institute of International Affairs, London, November.

Pluzhnikov, O. (2003). 'Climate policy of the Russian Federation – what next?', presentation at International Conference on 'Climate Policy after Marrakech: Toward Global Participation' (Honolulu: East-West Center), 4–6 September.

Pluzhnikov, O. (2005). *Realization of Kyoto Protocol in Russia in the Context of Environmental Policy.* Presentation, Montreal, December 2005. Available at *regserver.unfccc.int/seors/file_storage/us8ytzc5lyp23r0.pdf.*

Poole, J.B. and R. Guthrie (eds) (1996). *Verification 1996: Arms Control, Peacekeeping and the Environment* (Boulder, CO: Westview Press).

Rector, L. (2004). 'GHG Offset Limitations Undermine US Program Purposes', in Dornau (ed.), *Greenhouse Gas Market 2004,* pp. 81–2.

Reinaud, J. (2003). *Emissions Trading and its Possible Impacts on Investment Decisions in the Power Sector* (Paris: IEA).

RES (2003). *The Energy Strategy of Russia until 2020.* Moscow. Available at *http://www.mte.gov.ru/docs/32/189.html.* In Russian.

Rosendahl, R. (1996). 'Carbon taxes and the impacts on oil wealth', *Journal of Energy Finance and Development* 1(2), pp. 223–34.

Springer, U. (2003). 'The market for tradable GHG permits under the Kyoto Protocol: a survey of model studies', *Energy Economics* 25, pp. 527–51.

Stern, J. (2005). *The Future of Russian Gas and Gazprom* (Oxford: Oxford University Press).

Tangen, K., A. Korppoo, V. Berdin, T. Sugiyama, C. Egenhofer, J. Drexhage, O. Pluzhnikov, M. Grubb, T. Legge, A. Moe, J. Stern and K. Yamaguchi (2002), *A Russian Green Investment Scheme: Securing Environmental Benefits from International Emissions Trading,* Climate Strategies. Available at *http://www.climate-strategies.org/gisfinalreport.pdf.*

UNFCCC (1997). *The Kyoto Protocol.* Articles 6.1, 12.3 and 17.

UNFCCC (2000). *The Expert Review of the Second Russian National Communication*, FCCC/IDR.2/RUS. Available at *http://unfccc.int/resource/docs/idr/rus02.pdf*.

UNFCCC Secretariat (2004). 'Meeting eligibility requirements', presentation at the First Workshop on Implementation of Article 6, Session 4, held in Moscow, 26 May. Available at *http://unfccc.int/sessions/workshop/260504/agenda.html*.

Vasiliev, S.V. and G.V. Safonov (2003). 'The Kyoto Protocol and Russian business', *Bulletin Towards a Sustainable Russia*, No. 25 (Moscow: Centre for Russian Environmental Policy).

Williamson, R. (2004). *Climate Change: What Needs to be Done in North and South*, Wilton Park Paper, Conference Report, Wilton Park, Steyning.

World Bank (2003). *Russian Economic Report, August 2003*. Available at *www.worldbank.org.ru*.

WWF Russia (2003). 'WWF Russia analysis of publications and personal communications', presentation at side event at UNFCCC COP9, 8 December.

Yamin, F. and J. Depledge (2005). *The International Climate Change Regime: A Guide to Rules, Institutions and Procedures* (Cambridge: Cambridge University Press).

Zelinsky, A. (2003). 'Emissions trading system in RAO UES reform', presentation at side event held at COP9, Milan, 8 December. Available at *http://www.ieta.org/About_IETA/IETA_Activities/COP9/Dec8/IETA_COP9_Dec8_RAO.ppt#2*.

Zelinsky, A. (2004). 'Kyoto flexible mechanisms: perspectives for Russian industry', presentation in Brussels to the Committee of Industry, External Trade, Research and Energy of the European Parliament, 26 April. Available at *http://www.europarl.eu.int/hearings/20040426/itre/zelinsky_ en.pdf*.

INDEX

Page numbers in *italic* denote figures/tables

Other Titles in this Series

MIKE BARTLETT

Mike Bartlett's plays include *An Intervention* (Paines Plough/ Watford Palace Theatre); *Bull* (Sheffield Theatres/Off-Broadway); *Medea* (Glasgow Citizens/Headlong); *Chariots of Fire* (based on the film; Hampstead/West End); *13* (National Theatre); *Love, Love, Love* (Paines Plough/Plymouth Drum/Royal Court); *Earthquakes in London* (Headlong/National Theatre); *Cock* (Royal Court/Off-Broadway); *Artefacts* (Nabokov/Bush); *Contractions* and *My Child* (Royal Court).

He was Writer-in-Residence at the National Theatre in 2011, and the Pearson Playwright-in-Residence at the Royal Court Theatre in 2007. *Cock* won an Olivier Award for Outstanding Achievement in an Affiliate Theatre in 2010. *Love, Love, Love* won the TMA Best New Play Award in 2011. *Bull* won the same award in 2013.

Directing credits include *Medea* (Glasgow Citizens/Headlong); *Honest* (Northampton Royal & Derngate) and *Class* (Tristan Bates).

He has written seven plays for BBC Radio, winning the Writers' Guild Tinniswood and Imison prizes for *Not Talking*, and his three-part television series, *The Town*, was broadcast on ITV1 in 2012 and nominated for a BAFTA for Breakthrough Talent.

He is currently developing television projects with the BBC, ITV, Big Talk, and Drama Republic, and under commission from Headlong Theatre, Liverpool Everyman and Playhouse, Hampstead Theatre, and the Royal Court Theatre.